PRAISE FOR *IN THE LOTUS OF THE HEART* ...

"A deep, wise, and wonderful exploration of the Vedanta path for relationships, both with yourself and with others. In this book, Shubhraji provides everything you need to create healthy, fulfilling relationships, using ancient wisdom, beautiful stories, tools, and exercises. This book is a must read for those on a serious spiritual journey."

—Arielle Ford
Author of *Wabi Sabi Love* and *The Soulmate Secret*

"*In the Lotus of the Heart* is a profound and inspiring lesson in healing our love, lives, and ourselves by using ancient spiritual wisdom. I recommend it wholeheartedly."

—Brenda Wade, PhD
Author of *Love Lessons* and
99 Things You Wish You Knew before Falling in Love

"*In the Lotus of the Heart* is a wonderful book pointing readers to the essential ingredient in having successful and enriching relationships as well as getting in touch with what is best and highest in them. Using beautiful quotes from scriptures and sages along with excellent practical advice, it shows the way to the path of lasting love. We highly recommend this book to anyone seeking more fulfilling, enlightened relationships."

—Drs. Evelyn and Paul Moschetta
Marriage counselors and authors of *The Marriage Spirit* and
Are You Roommates or Soul Mates?

"Creating and maintaining loving relationships requires energy and dedication. In this book, Shubhraji dives deep into Vedanta and comes up with refreshing insights that help us effectively invest that energy and focus our dedication. Using simple stories, folk wisdom, and teachings of contemporary wise men and women, Shubhraji skillfully illustrates how awareness of our true inner selves enables us to succeed in our pursuit of joyful, positive, and sustainable relationships. I would highly recommend this poignant book to anyone seeking the freedom to fully enjoy the depth and beauty of their relationships."

—Vatsala Sperling, MS, PhD, PDHom, CCH, RSHom (NA)
Coauthor of *For Seven Lifetimes: An East-West Journey to a Spiritually Fulfilling and Sustainable Marriage*

"If you want to live a more loving life, read this book! *In the Lotus of the Heart*, a refreshing and innovative book, reminds us that we are the ultimate expression of love."

—Marci Shimoff
Author of the #1 *New York Times* bestseller *Happy for No Reason*, *Love for No Reason*, and *Chicken Soup for the Woman's Soul*

"Shubhraji examines the web of relationships in simple and effective ways, giving insightful tools to the reader that benefit every complex sphere of relationship within the world. I highly recommend this book; it is a wonderful lens on the core issues in relationships."

—Boman Irani, actor

In the
Lotus of the Heart

The Essence
of
Relationships

Shubhraji

NAMAH
Woodstock, New York

Published by: Namah
PO Box 1064
Woodstock, NY 12498
www.inthelotusoftheheart.com

Editor: Ellen Kleiner
Book design and production: Ann Lowe
Cover design: Ann Lowe

First Edition

Printed in the United States of America

Publisher's Cataloging-in-Publication Data

Shubhraji.
    In the lotus of the heart : the essence of relationships / by Shubhraji.
Woodstock, NY : Namah, c2015.

      p. ; cm.

      ISBN: 978-0-9912578-6-7 (paperback)
      ISBN: 978-0-9912578-7-4 (eBook)
      Summary: Through the practice of conscious relationship, we
transform patterns that block love, allowing us to reconnect with
our authentic self: our source of love, joy, and peace.--Publisher.

      1. Self-actualization (Psychology) 2. Self-realization.
Self-esteem. 4. Interpersonal relations. 5. Man-woman
relationships. 6. Self-help techniques. 7. Life skills. I. Title.

BF637.S4 S58 2015   2013956686
158/.1-dc23   1405

1 3 5 7 9 10 8 6 4 2

Offered at the lotus feet of my guru,
H. H. Swami Chinmayananda (1916–1993),
with infinite love and reverence

ACKNOWLEDGMENTS

My special thanks to Nancy O'Connor, who helped organize my material and shape the content of this book. Her invaluable insights and guidance in writing the book, as well as reviewing and enhancing the presentation of material, have been of exceptional value throughout the production of this work. Her compassion, understanding, and dedication have made the process a joy. I will always cherish this relationship.

My deepest thanks to:

Ellen Kleiner, my editor and publishing coordinator, who has been a guiding light, bringing her knowledge and experience every step of the way;

Swami Akhandanandji Maharaj, who inspired me toward devotion and love for God and instilled in my heart the meaning of love and gentleness;

David Frawley (Pandit Vamdeva Shastri) for encouraging me to write a book on Vedanta;

My father, Prem Narain Tandon, who was in my life for a short time yet left an indelible mark, influencing me deeply by his love, integrity, and enthusiasm—a most remarkable man who knew how to nurture relationships;

My mother, Swarnlata, who was my best friend, encouraging me to build meaningful relationships in every sphere of my life;

My eldest sister, Neeruji, who introduced me to Vedanta and to my guru, Swami Chinmayananda, for her love and caring throughout my spiritual journey;

My sisters Preetaji and Rashmiji, my brother Peushji, and his wife Neluji for always supporting me and believing in me; also my brothers-in-law Ravindra Mehta, Gopal Kapoor, and Saurabh Shodhan;

My spiritual sister and friend, Rajpriya Bhuckory, who read each chapter with keen interest and gave meaningful suggestions;

Poonam and Naren Patni for their ongoing support of my work over the years;

Nurith and Bob Shamis for their generosity in supporting Vedanta and numerous projects of Namah;

Kamala, my childhood nanny, who inspired me through her selfless love during my early years and today watches over me from the other world;

My generous publication sponsors;

The wonderful team at Blessingway for their wisdom and creativity;

And all my students and friends around the world who have always supported my work and without whom this book would be incomplete.

CONTENTS

The real work is not to search for love; it's to dispel the illusions that blind us to our true identity.

Introduction

*I*N MY TEACHING, I travel all over the world and counsel people from varied cultures and backgrounds. Regardless of nationality, people everywhere talk to me about the same relationship issues. Many feel lonely; often they're alienated from loved ones because of seemingly irresolvable conflicts and communication problems; or they suffer in stale, loveless, or even abusive relationships. Yet, at the same time, almost everyone shares a desire for loving, fulfilling relationships and wants to learn ways to more skillfully relate to others.

As a species we're wired to reach out and relate to others. We crave connection, desiring to be seen and valued for who we are and held in a supportive web of community. But our approaches to establishing connection often leave us frustrated. We seek love or try to solve relationship problems using the same strategies that created those problems in the first place. We try to change others so they meet our expectations, or we adjust our personality, hoping to make ourselves more lovable.

A story about the Sufi fool Nasrudin illustrates our situation. Late one night a man came upon Nasrudin crawling around under a streetlight, looking for something on the ground.

"Nasrudin, what are you looking for?" the man asked.

"I've lost my house key," he answered. The man offered to help Nasrudin, and soon both of them were crawling around futilely searching every millimeter of ground for the key.

Almost an hour went by before the man thought to ask the obvious question, "Where exactly did you lose it?"

Nasrudin pointed toward the darkness and replied, "Over there, across the street."

"So why are you looking for it here?" the man inquired.

"Because this is where the light is," replied Nasrudin.

The purpose of this book is to help readers reconsider their approaches to finding and maintaining beneficial relationships. Is it possible we're crawling around the wrong sidewalk, seeking love in the well-lit places of familiar patterns and expecting others to fulfill our needs, without venturing into the lesser-known territory of our own being?

In answering this question through discussing various facets of relationships, I turn to the ancient Vedanta teachings, looking at what these writings have to say about our modern relationship challenges. Vedanta is a collection of texts written and compiled in India beginning around 1500 BCE. The word *Vedanta* comes from the Sanskrit root word *vid*, meaning to know. *Veda* means knowledge, and *anta* means end; *Vedanta*, then, means the knowledge that frees us from all limitation. Even though Vedanta teachings are thousands of years old, their advice is timeless; they apply as much in our age of hypercommunication and frenetic activity as they did when they were first written and compiled, for their subject of true self-knowledge is at the core of all human experience.

Vedanta is not a religion claiming exclusive insights into to truth; rather, it is a system of thought expansive enough to encompass the principles of all major religions and belief systems. It recognizes that the truth animating our lives is too vast to be contained in the teachings of any one religion. Vedanta teaches that the key we believe we're missing is always within us: our real nature is infinite, and we are already whole and complete.

Because we suffer from a constricted sense of who we are, we search for love to complete us. But the real work is not to search for love; it's to dispel the illusions that blind us to our true identity. The lotus of the heart, our source of innate love and happiness, has been obscured by notions of limitations acquired from our past impressions. These impressions exist as energetic knots called *vasanas*. We can find freedom only when we release the knots. In doing so, we transcend the barriers blocking our innate capacity to love as well as our ability to experience our own divine essence and that of others. Relationships reveal the ways in which we sabotage love. Our fears, insecurities, aggression, cravings, inattention, and false images all surface in the mirror of relationships, so in facing them we can confront the barriers blocking our innate capacity to love.

Relationships, then, serve as a vital tool for neutralizing the effects of past conditioning, even those embedded in our cellular memories. Because outer conflicts reflect inner states, as we work through our difficulties in relationships we move toward greater internal integration. The image of the lotus flower, which both flowers and fruits, informs this process. Just as the budding lotus is nourished by the mud from which it grows, our limitations and challenges fuel our journey of discovering our innate capacity to love. As we recognize our wholeness and our essence as love, deeper dimensions of our personality begin to bloom and we experience greater harmony in our relationships.

Although intimate relationships are often the focus of relationship discussions, this book provides a perspective that can be applied to all relationships. Vedanta views everyone as living within a web of deeply connected relationships. A baby, even while in the uterus, develops a deep relationship to her mother. And the mother is connected to the external world through an intricate network of relationships consisting of family, friends, community, culture, and the natural world sustaining her life. So the baby, through the mother, is already connected to the world months before birth; and after birth the network expands. We're always in relationship, connected to one another, our towns or cities, our families, natural life forms, even the cup from which we drink our morning coffee or the shoes we put on our feet—and we're connected to the divine source of our being.

The relationship between an individual, the world, and the divine source of our being is like a cotton cloth on which a decorative pattern is woven; our attention focuses on the pattern, but the pattern depends on the cloth. Vedanta asks us to shift our attention to the cloth—our divine essence— the essential core possessed by everyone, called the Self in the Chandogya Upanishad. All of us are looking for love, recognition, and acknowledgment through the web of our relationships. But we focus so much on the external pattern—circumstances—that we ignore our own essence of divine love. Vedanta teaches a way to end such misconceptions and redefine who we truly are. Through self-knowledge, we learn to function via a new vision beyond our mental projections, based on recognition of our inner perfection. Self-knowledge also teaches us that our varied relationships all reflect different manifestations of an energy propelling us toward wholeness and peace.

This book lays out an accessible framework for approaching our inner life and our relationships. It is based on Vedanta's practical ways of living rooted in a deep experience of our true nature, which allow us to nurture our relationships with others. It increases our awareness of interconnection with other people and life-forms due to our common divine essence—our Self—a perspective that supports compassion and peace. As expressed in the Chandogya Upanishad, our divine essence, our true nature that helps us create loving relationships, exists within the lotus of the heart:

The Self is hidden in the lotus of the heart.
Those who see themselves in all the creatures go
day by day into the world of Brahman hidden
in the heart. Established in peace, they rise
above body consciousness to the supreme

light of the Self. Immortal, free from fear, this Self is Brahman, called the True. Beyond the mortal and the immortal, he binds both worlds together. Those who know this live day after day in heaven, in this very life.[1]

PART ONE

Uncovering the True Self

When we stop clinging to the mud of our thoughts, feelings, and desires, and allow our minds to become calm, the lotus in our hearts—our true selves—blossoms.

1

Seeking Treasure in the Lotus of the Heart

YOUR VISION WILL BECOME CLEAR ONLY
WHEN YOU CAN LOOK INTO YOUR OWN HEART.
WHO LOOKS OUTSIDE, DREAMS;
WHO LOOKS INSIDE, AWAKES.

—Carl Jung

*T*HE SEARCH FOR LOVE is fraught with difficulty, and more often than not "true love" turns out to be elusive. We are all familiar with the story of two lovers finally finding each other following an epic search, only to face other's challenges due to differences in their personal circumstances or dreams. For example, the woman wants to settle down in a small town close to her family while the man dreams of living in Tokyo. He doesn't always listen to her, or he's not as assertive as she'd like him to be; she's too emotional, or not emotional enough. There are countless variations on the scenario. A few lucky couples seem to sail happily through their lives enjoying loving, fulfilling relationships, but most people find that relationships are difficult and love presents constant challenges.

THE SOURCE OF TRUE LOVE

An Indian creation story explains why people have so much trouble finding lasting love. According to the story, God, after he finished creating the universe, wanted to give human beings the precious gift of love and happiness. But as their creator he also understood human psychology and knew people would take for granted anything they didn't have to struggle to get. So he decided to hide his gift where they would have to work to find it.

God consulted with his helpers, asking for ideas about hiding places. One of them suggested the ocean floor; another proposed outer space. But God knew that humans, with their insatiable desire to conquer the external world, eventually would be able find his gift even in the depths of the ocean or the vastness of space. Finally someone suggested the most obvious place—the heart.

Immediately, God recognized the brilliance of this idea. People would scurry around searching for love everywhere in the external world; and their own hearts, at the center of their beings, would be the last place they would look. If, after searching the entire universe and still failing in their quest, they thought to look within themselves, they would find the source of love. With that discovery, they could build the kind of relationships they yearned for. And after working so hard to find it, they would deeply value the treasure of their own hearts.

As the story describes, the treasure we seek is always with us—in our own hearts. Once we understand this, we can stop frittering away our energy in a futile quest looking outside ourselves for happiness. When we come to know ourselves as the source of love, that love spills out to other people, and joy animates our relationships.

Verse I–ii-20 from the *Kathopanishad* identifies that source of love within our hearts as the atman, or the Self.

> The atman that is subtler than the subtlest,
> and greater than the greatest,
> is seated in the cavity of the heart of each living being.
> He who is free from willing and wishing,
> with his mind and senses composed,
> beholds the majesty of the Self
> and becomes free from sorrow.[1]

This verse describes the essence of Vedanta—the source of love as the true self, which is the birthright of every human being, and the divine essence that needs nothing else to illuminate its existence. Different traditions use various terms to describe this essential aspect within the heart—the true self, the soul, the atman, Buddha nature, Christ consciousness, higher power—all of which identify the true self as the source of love. People who discover this treasure are released from searching and freed from sorrow. The great Indian spiritual teacher Ramana Maharshi tells us, "Happiness is the very nature of the self; happiness and the self are not different. There is no happiness in any object in the world."[2]

But even though the object of our longing lies right within our own hearts, we are conditioned to look for it in the external world. Oblivious to our inner treasure, we search for love as if window-shopping for the right person who will bring us happiness, in the same way we look for the right fabric for our living room couch. Or we try to "reupholster" the people already in our lives so they better fit our image of who we think they should be. Regardless of our particular situation, our basic strategy is to look outward for love but ignore the foundation of our own beings.

A story from Vedanta writings, "The Tenth Man," illustrates how such external focus is nothing new. In ancient India, ten young men from the same village were sent to study Vedanta in a guru's home. After a few days, they knew that a festival was to be held in their village so they pleaded with their guru to allow them to go back. Because the village was a long distance from the guru's home, he worried about their safety while traveling. But the most responsible student volunteered to lead the group and ensure their safe arrival, so the guru reluctantly agreed to let them go.

The group set off and eventually came to a river swollen by recent rains, which they had to cross to reach their village. The leader instructed them to hold hands and carefully wade across the river. Although the men tried their best to stay together, the raging current separated the group and swept them in different directions.

As they arrived on the other side of the river, the leader counted to make sure all ten students had made it safely across. To his dismay, he found only nine of them. Hoping he had made a mistake, he had the men line up and counted once more. Still, there were only nine. Every student double-checked by counting again, but they all confirmed the leader's count.

In a panic the students, convinced that one of them had been swept away by the current, ran off in different directions looking for their lost friend. Meanwhile, the leader stood still, fighting back tears while thoughts of disaster raced through his mind. He pictured the student being dragged under the water by the strength of the current, struggling in vain to stay afloat. He imagined the man's parents sobbing when they heard the news. He thought of how his guru had trusted him to make sure everyone remained safe. Finally, no longer able to hold back his tears he began wailing.

An old man, who had been watching from the shade of a nearby tree, approached him. The leader told him the entire story and ended by saying, "I volunteered to take charge. Now one of us has drowned, and it's my fault."

"Don't worry," the old man said, "I can find the tenth man. Call the rest of the students together and have them line up." The leader did as he was told.

The old man counted, "One, two, three, four, five, six, seven, eight, nine…" To the last in line he said, "You are the tenth man. Like the others, when you counted earlier you had forgotten to include yourself."

The students all looked stunned then burst out laughing. In forgetting to include themselves they had come to believe that one of them had gone tragically missing.

This story illustrates the human tendency to look outside ourselves to find whatever we think is missing. Our modern consumer culture bombards us with messages promising happiness from the external world, so it's not surprising that's where we look. But this story takes place in ancient India, a more inwardly focused culture; and the young men are students of Vedanta who presumably have not only learned the value of looking within but also practiced techniques for doing so. Yet even here the tendency is to look to the external world. Love is the very core of who we are, but unaware of this essential aspect of ourselves we run around searching for it, assuming it is missing from our lives.

SELF-KNOWLEDGE: THE FOUNDATION OF RELATIONSHIPS

If we want to experience genuine love, we must overcome this tendency to look to the external world for it. Love is found within us, and all loving relationships rest on our capacity to experience our true selves as whole and complete.

When we turn inward, we eventually discover a happiness independent of external circumstances or people, and we're freed from craving external objects. We discover we already are the love we have been yearning to find; and when we know ourselves as love, the joy that has escaped us flows forth.

The Vedanta texts say that we already are what we seek and because we don't see ourselves fully we cling to fragments of our identity—bits of thoughts, feelings, and desires—patching them together into a quilt we call "me."

But because our thoughts, feelings, and desires change constantly, these fragments of identity lack coherence, causing us to suffer from a chronic sense of incompleteness.

Feeling ourselves inadequate, we are driven by habitual patterns that Vedanta calls *vasanas*, which compel us to race after our desires in misguided attempts to achieve wholeness. We strive for money, position, power, possessions, and new relationships. But after obtaining what we want we experience only momentary happiness; then the nagging sense of insecurity again arises. None of these transitory acquisitions provides a sense of sustained joy because we are searching for love and happiness in the external world rather than in our own hearts.

Who are we really? We are more than our accomplishments, and the masks we wear are only limited expressions of our beings. We are not only the roles we play: mother, father, lawyer, artist, waiter, or gardener. Nor are we the kaleidoscope of attributes with which we identify: loving, angry, intelligent, insecure, clumsy, creative, anxious, confident, beautiful, or ugly. Through Vedanta's path of self-knowledge, we learn to look beyond our self-images, see ourselves with new eyes, and, transcending our mental projections of personal identity, discover our multidimensionality.

REALIZING WE ARE THE LOVE WE SEEK

When we know our true selves, we see nothing is missing: we are the love we seek. This essential state within each person is perfect. As Jesus put it, "The kingdom of heaven is within you" (Luke 17:21). Our fixation on thoughts, feelings, and desires—our mistaken identity—obscures who we really are. Our nature is like a lake on a stormy day. Wind stirs up the mud, obscuring the reflection of the silvery moon. But once the mud settles to the bottom the water reveals its purity, and the moon is clearly reflected. When we stop clinging to the mud of our thoughts, feelings, and desires, and allow our minds to become calm, the lotus in our hearts—our true selves—blossoms.

Every one of us has a true self connected to the essence of all creation whether or not we are conscious of this inner treasure. Verse II-ii-2 from the *Kathopanishad*, poetically translated by Eknath Easwaran, states:

The Self is the sun shining in the sky,
The wind blowing in space; he is the fire
At the altar and in the home the guest;
He dwells in human beings, in gods, in truth,
And in the vast firmament; he is the fish

Born in water, the plant growing in the earth,
The river flowing from the mountains.
For this Self is supreme![3]

One reality connects all beings and life-forms, but it manifests in countless ways, such as sun, wind, fire, lichens, skunks, roses, humans, rocks, phytoplankton, and quarks. Just as gold may take a number of forms—wedding rings, Olympic medals, coins, and crucifixes—the gold of universal consciousness manifests in an infinite variety of forms.

Our true, or authentic, self is connected with all life. This means that our spiritual dimension isn't separate from our everyday existence, or locked in some special beautiful box engraved with sacred symbols that we take out only at special times. Whether we are aware of it or not, we are that divine self all the time—day after day, even as we wash the breakfast dishes, drive in heavy traffic in pouring rain, argue with a friend, cry at a funeral, or wait in line at a grocery store. When we become fully aware of this ever-present power, confidence and understanding pervade all aspects of our lives. We comprehend that we don't need to change ourselves to fit an ideal image; we only need to live from our hearts.

People who live from a deeply felt sense of wholeness don't depend on others' opinions or approval to know who they are. Our true selves have no need for approval and can never be rejected. This sense of steadfast presence imparts confidence and an ongoing understanding that gives people like Martin Luther King and Mohandas Gandhi the courage to challenge widely accepted conventions and institutions such as racism, colonial rule, and the caste system.

A simple example of this kind of confidence is seen in Gandhi's decision to wear homespun Indian cotton clothes rather than the imported British suits in vogue at the time. He didn't worry that people wouldn't like him because of the way he dressed; he wasn't afraid of being rejected for improper behavior. Because he was motivated by his inner truth and dedication to empower the ordinary people of India to reclaim their dignity and self-sufficiency, other people's judgments were irrelevant.

True spiritual confidence grounded in self-realization gives us freedom and spontaneity. Life becomes play, and relationships become joyful interactions rather than complex undertakings. We know we are much more than the outfits we wear or the roles we play. We don't worry about the impression we're making; we act spontaneously with love and joy.

When we experience our wholeness, mental energy previously used to maintain a certain self-image is released. We stop trying to project an idealized image of ourselves; we are no longer driven by our self-created dramas; and we have more energy to focus on other people. We then expe-

rience the basis for healthy, fulfilling relationships—a sense
of completeness, peace, and love.

SEEING THE TRUE SELF OF OTHERS

As we come to know our own true selves, we recognize
the true selves of others, as well. The people in our life—our
partner, our children, the mailman, the eight-year-old girl
who lives down the street, our friends, the homeless woman
asking for help, the grumpy bus driver, our apparent enemies,
the countless people we pass on the street—all share the
same essence of divinity. Differences of social status, nationality, gender, sexual orientation, political beliefs, and religious
affiliations remain, but we can see through these to our
common core. What connects us is more fundamental and
powerful than surface features and personalities.

When we start to see the true selves of others, we recognize that common core more often. Daily domestic squabbles
become lighter. A woman may still be irritated by the way
her husband throws wet towels on the bathroom floor, but
she also remembers that he is a human being worthy of
respect. Such understanding can help soothe her annoyance
enough so the bathroom doesn't become a battleground
and so she can speak about soggy towels from a place of
love. Even if only one person in a relationship acts from such
understanding, the relationship will become more loving.

RELATIONSHIPS AS A PATH FOR
SPIRITUAL DEVELOPMENT

One of my students told me about an incident reflecting a change in how he related to his partner. He'd been feeling angry at his girlfriend and had almost gotten into a fight with her. He had made a passing comment, and she had unleashed a barrage of critical remarks, leaving him hurt and angry. He had started to react, but in a flash he remembered the teachings: you are much more than your thoughts and feelings; at your core, you are free. As a result, he stopped feeling threatened by her words and began listening to her without defending himself or getting angry. This was a significant departure from his previous impulsive behavior. He had reflected on his true nature and reaffirmed it. He had seen, in the end, that he and his partner shared the same essence of divinity. He had understood her frustration with him at a human level, and acceptance had come over him, allowing him to let his anger go. The next day his girlfriend admitted that she had been hard on him, and they were able to iron out their differences in a conscious way.

This example shows the practical value of introspection for building joyful relationships, which is a teaching of Vedanta. When we aspire to remain conscious on a regular basis, if a conflict arises we remember our connection with our true selves. Then relationships, valuable in themselves, also become essential to our spiritual development.

It may seem relatively simple to connect with our divine essence when sitting by a mountain stream in the midst of a pine-scented forest or when meditating in a beautiful, quiet room with burning incense and sacred images. The test comes when dirty, wet towels obstruct the path to the toilet or an onslaught of critical words is directed at us. Each time we remember to focus inward rather than reacting, we soften another hard edge of the ego and uncover love.

When we awaken to our true selves, we find a greater capacity to love. Love is its own fulfillment: the more we love, the more we become filled with love. When we are able to forget about our own agenda and truly care for others, we become animated by an ongoing sense of joy. As we relate to others with love, we help them grow and obtain a greater capacity to love as well, and that love, in turn, is reflected back to us.

LOVE WITHOUT EXPECTATIONS

So often we give to others with the expectation of getting something in return. If we are nice to someone, compliment them, give them gifts, or take care of them, we expect they'll do the same for us—and if they don't we become resentful. However, such an attitude is more like an investment strategy than love. One person may create a diversified portfolio: 30 percent to her partner, 20 to the children, 20 to the extended family, 20 to friends, 10 to casual acquaintances. Another person may put 100 percent of his stock in his immediate family. Regardless of the strategy, things are fine as long as there is a return on the investment of generosity and care. But when the investment isn't paying off and our people aren't acting as we expect them to, we moan about the ingratitude of our stocks. This kind of "caring" is closer to manipulation than to genuine love. As the poet Kahlil Gibran put it, "Love gives naught but itself and takes naught but from itself. Love possesses not, nor would it be possessed, for love is sufficient unto love."[4]

THE QUALITIES OF LOVE

I had the good fortune to study with a great spiritual master in India named Swami Akhandanandaji Maharaj, whose teachings about love provide a refreshing alternative to the investment-strategy style of "love." He once said that our love should contain three essential qualities: it should be intense, soft and gentle, and playful.

Love should be intense. Even if there are many reasons for it to break—relationships can be so fraught with conflict and difficulty that there are no shortages of such reasons—love should stand firm, cemented in the values that connected the people in the first place. Love built from the foundation of the true self has the resiliency to weather the inevitable irritations and stresses of life and any unmet expectations. It remains steady even when the markets are down.

Love should be soft and gentle. To describe this quality of love, my teacher used the analogy of ghee—clarified butter—which melts with ease. This gentle, almost fluid quality has the power to resolve conflicts. Ghee-like love arises spontaneously from the heart and flows through our whole being, increasing our capacity for love.

Finally, love should be playful. In any kind of relationship an element of playfulness affirms the bonds between people and creates a mood of lightness. Laughter and well-intentioned teasing enable us to experience each other in a more authentic way. Playfulness shakes up our identification with the ego, serves as an antidote for the common tendency to take things too seriously, and enables us to freely express the joy and creativity inherent in our relationships.

The teachings of Vedanta provide tools to free us from illusions obscuring the love within us. We don't need to acquire love; we don't have to trade the mask of our personality for a prettier version; we don't need a face-lift or a better online dating site. By turning inward, letting go of what we think we know, and giving up our illusions and selfish desires, we can find the love that is hidden in the lotus of the heart. The Sufi poet Rumi summed up the inner love and self-realization that is the foundation for relationships:

> The minute I heard my first love story,
> I started looking for you, not knowing
> how blind that was.
> Lovers don't finally meet somewhere.
> They're in each other all along.[5]

EXERCISES

1. Close your eyes, tune into your inner experience, and ask yourself, "Who am I?" Watch your breath for a few seconds, becoming aware of each inhalation and exhalation. Then become conscious of any thoughts or feelings that arise, and ask yourself, "Who is thinking these thoughts? Who is feeling these emotions?" Continue observing your thoughts and emotions without resisting or manipulating them. Then ask yourself, "Am I separate from these thoughts and emotions? Who am I?" Say to yourself, "I am the light that illuminates my thoughts. I am the light that illuminates my emotions."

2. Think of several people with whom you have a relationship, some close and others not so close. Next, envision each of these people as an embodiment of divine essence despite their shortcomings or your level of affection for them.

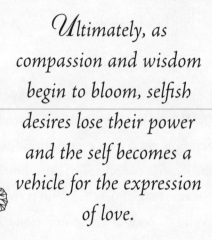

Ultimately, as compassion and wisdom begin to bloom, selfish desires lose their power and the self becomes a vehicle for the expression of love.

2

Out of the Mud

RECOGNIZING *VASANAS* AND EGOCENTRIC DELUSIONS

YOUR TASK IS NOT TO SEEK FOR LOVE, BUT MERELY TO SEEK AND FIND ALL THE BARRIERS WITHIN YOURSELF THAT YOU HAVE BUILT AGAINST IT.

—Helen Schucman

WE ALREADY ARE THE LOVE WE SEEK, but we can only experience this love when we stop blocking its flow. We have all erected barriers to resist the flow of love, which we must discover and eliminate in order to fully experience love.

THE BARRIER OF SEPARATION

One of the most fundamental barriers blocking the flow of love is the conviction that we are separate from others and unconnected to the rest of life. As long as we believe ourselves to be separate individuals, we search for love outside ourselves, hoping someone else will heal our feeling of isolation so we can experience love. In attempting to satisfy our yearning for unity, we try to seduce, manipulate, or over-power others to meet our needs and satisfy our desires. But in this misguided quest for love we lose the spontaneous joy of a loving connection.

The perception of separateness develops early in child-hood and over time becomes increasingly strong. As long as her needs are met, ten-month-old Ana feels intimately connected to whatever appears in her life. She views every-thing she encounters—her mother, the stuffed toy monkey in her crib, the breeze blowing against her cheek while she rides in her stroller—as who she is.

But this experience of unity is short-lived. By the time Ana is four years old she no longer defines herself by the events that occur in her life but rather as her body, emo-tions, desires, and the messages she has internalized about herself from interactions with others, especially her parents. She now sees her mother as a powerful person separate from herself, whom she needs in order to survive. Similarly, she believes she needs her beloved toy monkey in order to feel secure. At night she feels alone and is frightened of the dark, so she sleeps with her monkey and arrives at pre-school clutching it tightly, afraid the other children will take it. Although Ana is not consciously aware of her insecurity, it exerts a powerful influence on her thoughts and behavior. Eventually she will outgrow her monkey, but her underlying need for security will remain a strong aspect of her psyche, as will the subconscious belief that she is incomplete and lacking, both of which will affect her relationships.

VASANAS

Each of us has a particular variety of *vasanas* that gives our personality its unique blueprint, colors our view of the world, and shapes what we think and how we act. *Vasanas* are deep unconscious imprints in the psyche—latent tendencies stored in our memory that influence our thoughts and feelings and ultimately drive our behavior. In directing our thoughts, feelings, and actions, *vasanas* create habits and desires. One person may try to overcome a *vasana* of limitation by developing her athletic abilities; another, by searching for the elusive perfect partner. Feeling limited and incomplete, we compensate by fulfilling desires according to our temperament.

When we repeatedly act on such desires, our *vasanas* are strengthened and the habitual patterns become more deeply ingrained. Over time, *vasanas* may become so powerful that they drive us compulsively, obscuring our inherent state of wholeness and interconnection. For example, four-year-old Ana's ferocious attachment to her toy monkey is an early manifestation of her *vasana* of insecurity. In her teenage years the pattern takes a different form, and she becomes obsessed with buying clothes, hoping that wearing the latest fashion will make her feel good enough. A stylish new dress gives her a temporary surge of confidence, but within days the dress seems ordinary and becomes just another piece of clothing hanging in the overstuffed closet of an insecure young woman. As years go by, Ana spends thousands of her hard-earned dollars on clothes.

A *vasana* can be either negative or a positive, depending on how a person chooses to act on it. Someone suffering from a *vasana* of anxiety may want to suppress his awareness of it. As soon as he experiences anxiety, he craves a shot of whiskey. The drink temporarily numbs his anxiety; but when the effect of the alcohol wears off, the anxiety reemerges stronger than ever. By acting on his desire for alcohol, he has strengthened the *vasana*, and now he even more desperately wants a drink—so he downs another shot, continuing the cycle. Eventually, as anxiety becomes a dominant force in his consciousness and alcohol a daily habit, he's filled with guilt and shame. He withdraws from his family and friends, spending most evenings alone in the neighborhood bar. Someone else driven by a *vasana* of anxiety may instead choose not to act on it but rather observe its impact on her, so she seeks counseling, begins jogging, and takes up meditation. As a result, she becomes increasingly aware of how often anxiety drives her actions, causing her to avoid conflict and shut down in her relationships. Upon seeing these patterns, she begins to acknowledge their presence and make more conscious choices. Rather than allowing anxiety to rule her, she starts basing her actions on the needs of the situations in which she finds herself.

A positive effect of a *vasana* results from choosing to neutralize or wear out its power; a negative effect entails letting it impel us to action, thereby fueling the *vasana* and further obscuring our true selves veiled beneath it. A *vasana* becomes fueled in this way because each time it is reinforced by our actions it deepens the impression it leaves in the mind. Just as a car stuck in the mud and spinning its wheels will deepen the grooves, habitual actions and ruminations of the mind intensify *vasana* imprints so that over time they become more firmly embedded in the psyche. From a linguistic perspective, a *vasana* having a negative effect is known as a negative *vasana*, and one with a positive effect is called a positive *vasana*.

Although an increase in positive *vasanas* makes us better human beings, both types of *vasanas* distort reality by concealing the divine self. As my teacher, Swami Chinmayananda, explained, "*Vasanas* veil the divinity in us, and therefore they are known as ignorance. The pure, divine Self is our true nature, but due to our *vasanas* and consequent agitations of

the mind, we become ignorant of our true nature and identify ourselves with our personality and its limitations."[1]

VASANAS IN RELATIONSHIPS

Most people approach relationships from a sense of
inadequacy, looking for someone to make them feel complete. The problem is that this approach never really works:
the limited ego-self is constructed from a foundation of
transitory thoughts, emotions, and desires, so it always feels
inadequate and craves wholeness. Nobody—no matter how
loving, beautiful, creative, sexy, rich, or fascinating they may
be—can ever fill the void experienced by someone else.

For example, at age twenty-two Ana meets Ramon and
believes she has finally found the missing part of herself.
When she's with him, she feels safe, happy, and complete.
The couple spends every available minute together. They go
on long walks, talking for hours, sharing the details of their
lives. Through Ramon's eyes, Ana sees herself as beautiful,
desirable, and interesting. Ana has a part-time position in a
dance company and, to pay her bills, a second job waitress-
ing in an upscale restaurant. Ramon works as an accountant
in an established computer software company. Ana sees him
as practical and solid, qualities she feels she lacks. Above all,
he seems dependable, and when she is with him she feels
secure and cherished.

Ramon's *vasanas* are rooted in a sense of insecurity, as are Ana's, but for him they manifest in a need to control and strong ambition. He follows the same schedule every day, keeps his apartment meticulously clean, and tries to control his emotions at all times. Ana adds inspiration to his routine life. When he is with her, he sees the world in a new way. When they walk through the city, she points out things he's never noticed: cat prints in the mud, the shadow of a bare tree against a pale wall, the expression of rapture on a toddler's face as he tastes chocolate ice cream. Ana expresses the imaginative side of Ramon's personality, which he shut down many years ago due to his single-minded focus to get ahead. But as time goes on Ana and Ramon will never be able to adequately fill the voids in each other.

In the beginning of a relationship when two people connect, they experience a sense of wholeness. Life seems full and vivid. But the moment of fulfillment quickly slips away. The thoughts and feelings of the ego-centered self are continually shifting like foam on the surface of a vast ocean. One person forgets to call; the other feels insecure and anxious. Suddenly the tone of the relationship changes, and once they realize the initial magic of connection has faded they scramble to recreate it. Because they each believe their partner created their happiness, they expect their partner can make it return. But in reality, the capacity for joy lies within and was only temporarily activated by the other person.

Just as Ana at age four believed her toy monkey could make her safe, later she believes Ramon is the cause of her happiness. And once Ana loses the feeling of security and love she believes Ramon created, she becomes convinced she needs him even more for her to feel happy again and consequently wants more from him—more time together, more affection, more reassurance. She becomes obsessed with him, waiting for his calls, planning their time together, trying to find ways to look more beautiful and be more lovable.

Ramon then becomes unhappy. He thought Ana would provide an escape from his heavy responsibilities and the means to spontaneous joy. Instead, she has become another burden and a source of anxiety. He feels he should be able to make her happy, but as she continues to demand more attention he feels inadequate and irritated, and he pulls away.

THE SUFFERING DUE TO
ATTACHMENT AND ANGER

By seeking fulfillment from another person, we reduce that person to an object—someone who exists to fulfill our needs. For instance, rather than seeing our partner as a multifaceted human being, we project onto him what we believe we lack. As long as we attach to someone else, expecting him to complete us, we will be dissatisfied. Even if the most perfect, gorgeous, radiant god descended from heaven and showed up at our doorstep, we would feel incomplete. After a few days of ecstatic happiness, we would realize we still feel inadequate and our expectations have not been met. Then we would project our discontent on to him by becoming angry and finding fault with him.

In relationships, strong attachment can turn into obsessive desire. Desire rooted in unconscious *vasanas* contains expectations, either acknowledged or unacknowledged. When these expectations are not met, unfulfilled desire turns to anger. An undercurrent of anger can slowly poison love between two people. Unless the roots of anger are brought into consciousness and transformed through loving awareness, both people in the relationship will suffer. The Bhagavad Gita, in chapter 2, verses 62 and 63, describes the destructive cycle set in motion by attachment that leads to anger:

> When a man thinks of objects, attachment for them
> arises;
> from attachment desire is born; from desire arises anger ...
> From anger comes delusion; from delusion, loss of memory;
> from loss of memory, the destruction of discrimination;
> from destruction of discrimination, he perishes.[2]

In this destructive cycle set in motion by attachment, once anger arises relationships quickly deteriorate. The intense energy of anger takes over the mind and body, convincing the angry person of the rightness of her view. Her nervous system is flooded with stimulating chemicals, and she loses the ability to think clearly. When anger dominates the mind, the enraged person forgets about self-control, kindness, and long-term consequences; she suffers from "loss of memory . . . the destruction of discrimination."

A story about the Sufi fool Nasrudin illustrates the loss of memory and destruction of discrimination resulting from anger. One beautiful sunny morning Nasrudin was walking down the street bundled up in a heavy jacket when he passed a friend.

His friend stopped and asked, "Nasrudin, why on earth are you wearing that heavy jacket on such a lovely day?"

"I'll tell you," Nasrudin answered scowling, "if you promise to keep it a secret. You know that big idiot Ahmed. He's always coming up to me and slapping me on the back really hard. It hurts, and it infuriates me. I've asked him to stop, but he's such a dimwit he can't restrain himself. I'm going to teach him a lesson he won't forget."

"What are you going to do?" asked the friend.

"I've got a stick of dynamite hidden under this jacket,

strapped to my back. The next time that fool slaps me on the back he'll get his arm blown off," replied Nasrudin.

Nasrudin's unawareness of the consequences of his planned revenge seems ludicrous but is really not so far-fetched. He expects his friend to behave the way he wants him to. When his friend doesn't comply and Nasrudin's expectations are not met, he becomes angry, losing his ability to reason. When one person lashes out at another, he may cause injury, yet the one he damages the most is himself. In the constricted state of anger, he acts heedlessly, blind to the full consequences of his actions. When both people in a relationship become angry, the damage is compounded. Two people fueled by anger and acting without discrimination can cause each other great suffering, destroying what was once a loving relationship.

The root cause of this misery is the mistaken belief that the ego is the totality of who we are. Then by acting on our *vasanas* we reinforce that limited identity. Relationships based on the shaky foundation of an ego-centered self lead inevitably to insecurity and unrealistic demands and expectations. When expectations are not met, anger arises, and the ability to discriminate is lost. As long as consciousness is focused only on the small self and its stream of never-ending egocentric desires, we can never begin to know— let alone love—another person.

THE DISTORTED LENS OF *VASANAS*

In many relationships, *vasanas* act as a distorted lens through which one person projects desires onto another person, ignoring whatever doesn't fit their particular needs. When our perceptions are obscured by *vasanas*, we see others as we would like them to be. We want our partner to make us feel good, so we focus on his kindness and sense of humor, constructing an image of him as a patient, good-hearted man. Then when he shows us another side of his personality—by snapping at us when we buy the wrong kind of cookies, for instance—we become offended and indignant. Often people will leave relationships after decades, saying, "I never really knew my partner" or "My partner never understood me." We wonder what's happened to the sweet man we married.

A story from India provides a simple example of how *vasanas* shape our view of other people: A man was lying by the side of the road, and, within minutes, four different people passed him. The first person looked at the man and said, "A typical gambler! He spent the whole night in the casino, wasting his money and ruining his family. Now he's so exhausted he can't even make it home."

The second person stopped for a moment and said, "Poor guy, he must be ill." Then, remembering all he had to do that day, he added, "I better not disturb him. He needs to rest."

The third person barely looked at the man and turned away in disgust, saying, "Another filthy drunk who doesn't know when to stop."

The last person stopped, bowed to the man, and said, "To a saint, even the pavement is heaven. He can find God everywhere. How marvelous!"

Which man saw the reality of the situation? We don't know. Maybe none of them. The various interpretations tell us something about how each person's *vasana* colors his view of the world but little about the man lying on the sidewalk.

Because we interpret the world through the distorted lens of our *vasanas*, our desires shape how we see other people. We are attracted to individuals we believe will fulfill our desires, and we avoid or attack individuals who challenge them. Through such attraction and avoidance, we diminish our capacity to love and enjoy other people.

As soon as we judge a person, we reduce her to a projected image. Every human being is a mystery, a vast and complex universe, but if we believe our thoughts about other people, we undermine our ability to truly know them. If we can look at a friend, a child, or a lover without imposing our beliefs and judgments on them, even for a minute, we will realize that the person we thought we knew is more expansive than our constructed image of them. And if we can suspend our beliefs about ourselves we will understand that we, too, are infinitely more than our conditioned patterns. Walt Whitman clearly recognized this when he wrote, "I am vast. I contain multitudes."[3]

THE ILLUSORY SELF

From the perspective of higher consciousness, the limited ego-based self is an illusion—albeit a powerful one that compels us to want to preserve it at all costs. We define ourselves in certain ways according to our *vasanas*. For example, I consider myself a good tennis player, a friendly person, an animal lover, an outspoken individual with strong convictions about right and wrong, a person who values cleanliness and order. Because I believe in my self-created image, I then reinforce it by my actions, keeping my house immaculately clean and sweeping the sidewalk every morning and stopping to chat with neighbors when I take walks. I take pleasure in the well-kept houses on my street, but I'm offended by a house on the corner that has peeling paint and a dirty sidewalk, feeling a subtle distaste for whoever lives there. One morning the owner of this house walks out on his rickety porch and greets me with a smile. But because my perception of him is already distorted, colored by my *vasanas*, I'm not interested in knowing the owner of this shabby house, so I ignore his greeting and continue walking. My action is so automatic that I'm barely aware I've made the decision. But by shutting him out I shut out the possibility of shifting my habitual view of the world, opening to someone who challenges my values, and connecting with someone from whom I could learn.

Every day, I make hundreds of unconscious choices based on my *vasanas* and the distortions they impose, causing my mind to project. The resulting actions strengthen and perpetuate my egocentric personality. However, this "friendly" self who directs my actions—and who loves order, tennis, and animals—has no more reality than a cartoon character who turns out to be just a series of sketches put together to create an illusion of solidity. Nonetheless, until I question that identity I am bound by it, acting, often unconsciously, to fulfill its needs.

When we are in a dark theater watching a convincing film, we may experience a range of emotions—sadness, fear, relief, joy—and become fully absorbed in the world of the movie. Then stepping outside the theater into three-dimensional reality, we feel the summer heat and hear random snippets of conversation from people queued up for the next show, and the movie becomes only a memory. Similarly, when we wake up from the dream of our ego-centered selves reality reveals itself as vastly larger than the constricted world in which we'd been living.

Vedanta uses the analogy of a snake and a rope to show the illusory nature of the ego. A man is walking through a dense, dark forest when he sees a long, curved object and instantly recognizes it as a snake. He breaks out in a cold sweat, his heart pounds, his mouth goes dry, and his stomach churns. Suddenly, a person approaches and shines a flashlight on the object, revealing it to be a rope. The instant the light illuminates the rope the man wakes up to reality; in response, his breathing deepens, his nervous system calms, and he understands that his terror was his own creation.

The man's recognition of the snake as a rope is a pivotal moment. Until then, his mind has functioned to obscure understanding; but when the light of consciousness reveals reality the man sees how he distorts the world through his projections and creates his own suffering. Then he realizes he can decide to escape the prison of his illusions.

WAKING UP TO WHO WE ARE

Once the ego-based self gives up its struggle to maintain its illusions, the energy previously expended to meet self-centered needs is redirected toward transformation. And when the mind serves as an instrument for inner transformation, it begins to function in a positive way.

A person who feels secure in her true self doesn't have to demand that others meet her needs or expectations. With time and effort, she clearly understands that the snakes of her imagination are really ropes, and she doesn't need to project her fears or desires onto other people. In this context, the mind becomes an ally—rather than an obstacle—in engaging in loving relationships. As the Vietnamese Zen master Thich Nhat Hahn put it, the suffering of the ego-centered self "acts as a kind of mud to help the lotus flower grow."[4] Ultimately, as compassion and wisdom begin to bloom, selfish desires lose their power and the self becomes a vehicle for the expression of love.

Although the path to loving relationships requires energy and dedication, Vedanta assures us transformation is possible. In the Bhagavad Gita, chapter 6, verse 35, the daring warrior Arjuna complains to Krishna about the difficulty of subduing the turbulent mind, saying it is as difficult to control as the wind. Krishna answers, "Undoubtedly, O mighty-armed one, the mind is difficult to control and is restless; but by practice, O Son of Kunti, and by dispassion, it is restrained."[5]

Modern neuroscience is beginning to provide evidence in support of Krishna's claim. In recent years, a number of experiments using magnetic resonance imaging (MRI) have demonstrated the brain's ability to change in response to mental training in ways that can be measured. Researchers studying the effects of various spiritual practices on the brain have observed specific physiological alterations in particular regions of the brain. Although MRIs can't tell us how these changes within the brain affect people's personal experiences, research does show that people who engage in consistent, systematic spiritual training notice a reduction in anxiety, depression, and stress and an increase in self-awareness, ability to focus, calmness, and empathy.

Eliminating old habits of the mind takes time and effort. For example, an alcoholic may substitute a craving for recognition of her artistic talent for a craving for whiskey then stop drinking whiskey and develop her abilities as a painter. Certainly in doing this she is relatively better off. But as long as she is—in the words of the Bhagavad Gita (chapter 5, verse 12)—"impelled by desire and attached to the fruits"[6] she still suffers. When her paintings receive a negative review, she feels despondent. Then when her work is exhibited in a museum in her hometown, she is temporarily elated, but soon she feels dissatisfied and wants her work seen in Paris or New York. Her reactions are natural—elation and despondency, fear and attraction are part of the human emotional mandala—but she still suffers from her desires. Similarly, a couple can learn new ways to communicate, becoming more skillful at expressing emotions and resolving conflicts. But as long as the relationship is built only on the shaky foundation of ego-centered selves driven by desires, the source of deep love is obscured by the ego's distortions.

In charting out the path to loving relationships, Vedanta asks us to do more than substitute one habit for another. It directs us to go deeper and wake up to who we really are. While seeing ourselves as separate and incomplete, we are driven by desire and fear. We project into the future, trying to obtain whatever we think will make us happy, but this incessant striving blocks the wonder of the present moment. In squandering our mental energy obsessing about an imagined future, we fail to appreciate all that is in our midst.

Einstein described our illusion of separateness as a central issue of human existence: "A human being is a part of the whole called by us 'universe,' a part limited in time and space. He experiences himself, his thoughts and feelings as something separated from the rest—a kind of optical delusion of his consciousness. The striving to free oneself from this delusion is the one issue of true religion. Not to nourish the delusion but to try to overcome it is the way to reach the attainable measure of peace of mind."[7]

Better communication techniques or new activities may improve the quality of our relationships, but to know our true selves we need to make a radical shift. In Part Two of this book, we will explore ways to free ourselves of the delusions that prevent us from sustaining joyful relationships and also connect with the unshakable foundation of love—the true self.

EXERCISES

1. Identify three qualities you bring to relationships and three qualities you think you need from other people. Close your eyes, connect with the deepest part of yourself, and become conscious of your breath. Infuse yourself with the three things you believe you need from external relationships, and visualize these qualities filling you. As you continue this practice, you will realize that when you connect with your divine essence, or true self, your needs become fulfilled.

2. Identify two negative words or phrases that often arise during your daily interactions with others (examples: *fear, anger, jealousy, sense of being out of control, desire to be accepted, feeling misunderstood, sense of incompleteness, irritation at others*). Now choose a word or phrase to use as an antidote (examples: *trust, acceptance, confidence, courage, love*). The next time negative thoughts arise, practice replacing them with these positive words or phrases.

PART TWO

Paths of Awakening

*When we take our
emotions and thoughts to
be real and permanent,
we are powerless to
change our inner state.*

3

The Path of Awareness

SEEING THROUGH THE VEILS OF DELUSION

THE STATE OF SELF-REALIZATION . . . IS NOT ATTAINING SOMETHING NEW OR REACHING SOME GOAL WHICH IS FAR AWAY, BUT SIMPLY BEING THAT WHICH YOU ALWAYS ARE AND WHICH YOU ALWAYS HAVE BEEN. ALL THAT IS NEEDED IS THAT YOU GIVE UP YOUR REALIZATION OF THE NOT-TRUE AS TRUE.

—Ramana Maharshi

TUKARAM, AN INDIAN SAINT, was famous for mastering his emotions. He never got angry but remained calm regardless of what happened.

One day a despondent-looking man approached him for advice. "Please, tell me your secret," he begged. "My relationships are a mess. My wife constantly criticizes me. My son doesn't respect me, and my employees are a bunch of lazy fools. I spend most of my time arguing or feeling furious with everyone. How do you manage to stay calm all the time?"

For a moment, Tukaram just sat quietly looking at the man. Then, instead of answering his question, he said, "My

dear fellow, I must warn you. I'm going to tell you something you don't want to hear." He paused for a moment then
continued, saying: "In seven days you are going to die. I can
see this as clearly as the nose on your face. I will pray for
you, but no one can avert death. The best thing you can do
is go home and try to prepare yourself. If you come back in
six days, I'll give you a blessing."

When the man returned on the sixth day, his face was
serenely radiant. Tukaram looked at him and asked, "So
how did it go?"

"It was the best week of my life," the man answered.

"Did you get angry?" Tukaram asked.

"Of course not. How could I waste my time being angry
knowing I have so little time left?"

"But your nagging wife? Your disrespectful son? Your
lazy employees?"

"Everyone has changed. My family seems different,
and so do my employees. They are all wonderful, precious
people. If only I had been able to see them this way before
instead of being furious with them or taking them for
granted."

Many of us live like the man in the story. We focus on
people's flaws and take much for granted, acting as though
our lives will go on forever and the people we love will always
be there. Then the reality of death hits. Faced with the loss

of someone we love or our own death, we are shocked out of our habitual patterns; everything in the world looks more appealing, and we see people in a fresh way. Realizing our time is limited and the people we care about could disappear at any time, we speak from our hearts and connect more deeply with others.

But typically we don't sustain this awareness. The ingrained habits of a lifetime reassert themselves, and we retreat into a safer, more familiar world where death happens only to other people, at some other time and place.

THE TRANSFORMATIVE POWER OF AWARENESS IN RELATIONSHIPS

Tukaram's story shows how awareness can be a transformative gift. When the man returns home knowing death is near, his heart opens so he's able see the preciousness and beauty of the people in his life. He can see past his wife's nagging to recognize her vulnerability and love. She, in turn, feeling his warmth, becomes less critical of him and begins to treat him with tenderness.

Realizing how little time he has to spend with his son, the man stops lecturing him and becomes interested in finding out who he is. As he listens with awareness—rather than through a filter of preconceived assumptions and judgments—he hears an intelligent, thoughtful young man. Sensing his father's genuine interest in him, the son begins to speak honestly and share his feelings.

It is the prospect of impending death that jolts the man into increased awareness. Vedanta, however, teaches us that we don't have to be near death to appreciate and connect with other people. The Vedanta path presents a systematic method for doing this at any time in life by realizing our true selves and subsequently the true selves of others. And indeed, after being barraged with self-help books, seminars, and workshops promising instant happiness by changing our patterns, after a while we ourselves discover that instead we need to become less identified with them so we can know who we truly are.

Vedanta often refers to "pure consciousness"—awareness that is free and unchanging—which plays through the mind, emotions, and body, allowing us to think, feel, and act from a broader perspective. Typically, we aren't aware of this underlying pure consciousness and instead identify with our constantly changing thoughts, emotions, and desires, forging them into the deceptive identity we call "me." But once aware of the pure consciousness that permeates our being we can see the fabricated ego-centered self as the fictional creation that it is. Then, as we begin taking our ego-centered selves more lightly, our *vasanas* become less dominant; less enslaved by them, we begin to more freely choose our actions; and we start treating people more kindly, no longer compelled to lose our temper if they don't behave the way we want.

DEVELOPING AWARENESS THROUGH MEDITATION

To foster movement toward the freedom of pure consciousness, Vedanta presents a technique for lessening one's identification with the constructed "me" and diminishing the power of *vasanas*. The first step in this technique is to find a quiet place, sit with the spine upright, and close your eyes. Then simply observe all your thoughts and emotions as they arise, without attempting to analyze or change them. As I observe, I notice how busy and scattered my mind is. Thought after thought arises—I plan breakfast, replay an argument with my partner, think about work, remember an appointment, wonder how Congress will vote on a bill, feel a surge of anger about a traffic ticket, and worry about how much money is in my checking account. Then just as I'm about to race to the computer to check my bank balance, I remember my intention to observe my mind rather than allowing myself to be driven by thoughts and feelings. For a moment, I am able to watch my thoughts and emotions as they arise and vanish and recognize them as ephemeral events. When I allow my thoughts and emotions to be present without judging them, I notice how they lessen their control over me and eventually subside.

While observing, we try to let go of judgments and associations. We let the thoughts come and go and the emotions rise or fall, simply being aware of them. When the mind wanders, we focus again on the present moment and continue to just observe. The observer viewing these thoughts and emotions is pure consciousness, our true identity. The observer's ability to watch with nonattachment all the drama on the surface of the mind allows the mind to settle and clear. Through such observation and meditation we eventually connect to the most subtle layer of our being, which resides behind the movements of the mind—the source of our existence.

An Indian story illuminates this process. A man who was struggling with meditation asked his teacher for advice.

"What happens when you start to meditate?" his teacher asked.

The man explained that his beloved buffalo had died a few days before and that whenever he tried to meditate the buffalo would appear in his mind.

"Excellent," his teacher answered. "Remain focused on the buffalo. Ask yourself, 'What is the essence of the buffalo? Is it the bones of the buffalo? Is it the skin or the flesh? Or is it the breath? Is it the buffalo's love for its calf and the way it tenderly licks her? Is it the instinct that propels her to run from a tiger, or the joy she feels chewing her cud?' Once you've found the essence of the buffalo, come back and see me."

The man followed his teacher's instructions, examining each characteristic of the buffalo to see if he could pinpoint its essence. But as he persisted with this practice he became increasingly frustrated. No single characteristic or combination of characteristics seemed to reflect the essence of his beloved buffalo.

Finally he returned to his teacher and confessed, "I haven't been able to find the essence of the buffalo."

"Good," the teacher answered. "Now, you're ready to meditate on yourself. Ask yourself the same question, 'Who am I in my essence?'"

This time as the man meditated he quickly was able to see he was neither his physical characteristics nor his personality traits. Observing how his thoughts and emotions shifted from moment to moment, he began to sense the light of awareness illuminating those thoughts and emotions. As he questioned, "Who am I in my essence?" that light became stronger, and his thoughts and emotions seemed less solid until finally both he and the question dissolved into the light of pure consciousness.

CALMING THE MIND THROUGH
MANTRA CHANTING

Most people who practice meditation for any length of time discover the truth of Arjuna's complaint to Krishna about the mind being as difficult to control as a turbulent wind. Fortunately, Vedanta teaches how to use mantras as tools to focus the scattered mind and bring the mind and heart to a single point. A mantra is a sound, syllable, word, or group of words with the power to transform consciousness. The word *mantra* means "that which protects." A mantra protects us from negative influences, helps eliminate unwanted thoughts, assists us in focusing attention, and most importantly, strengthens our awareness of our true selves.

Hundreds of mantras are available for personal use, including, from the Hindu tradition, Om Gama Ganapatye Namah, Om Namah Shivaya, Om Namo Narayana, Om Sri Ramaya Namah, Om Sri Durgayai Namah, Om Sri Hanumate Namah, and Sri Krishna Sharanam Mamah. You are free to choose whichever one works for you. Alternatively, a knowledgeable teacher can help in the selection of an appropriate mantra and guide you in its recitation.

Most Eastern traditions designate specific time spans for chanting mantras: some of the most effective are seven, twenty-one, or forty days. A more sustained time frame, such as a year or several years, works even better. I know people, myself included, who have chanted the same mantra for thirty or forty years. The key is to develop the practice slowly.

A mantra should be chanted at least 10 times, but it's better to repeat it more often: 27, 54, or optimally, 108 times. The more a mantra is repeated, the more powerful it becomes. A mantra can be chanted aloud, softly, or silently. Sometimes people use rosary beads to help them; for example, the Hindu tradition advocates use of a rosary with 108 beads on a string.

Practitioners traditionally repeat the mantra at their meditation seat before meditation practice or prayer. Most mantras can be chanted at any time, preferably while sitting either on the floor or in a chair at an altar or in a fixed, quiet place in your home.

Mantra chanting, first and foremost, directs the mind to the chanting or the beads, and lessens the focus on scattered thoughts arising second by second. Chanting calms the mind, allowing us to experience connection with our deeper source, our true selves.

The repetition of mantras works this by slowly creating a groove within the mind, eradicating previous impressions that triggered negative thoughts and actions. Thus mantras act like cleansing spring rains, removing old debris and, all the while, slowly weakening *vasanas* and replacing them with positive vibrations. The beauty of this practice is its simplicity; anyone can experience the transformative effect of mantras.

Over time both the practice of meditation and the repetition of mantras helps release the subconscious material that scatters our energy and perpetuates old patterns. These are time-tested techniques for getting in touch with the true self.

OBSERVATION IN RELATIONSHIPS

As we learn to focus our minds, we become increasingly familiar with the negative and positive *vasanas* driving our thoughts, emotions, and actions. We start to see how our *vasanas* control us, influencing every facet of our lives, including restricting our freedom to think rationally and act authentically in relationships. When observation of our consciousness becomes an ongoing practice, we experience thoughts and emotions as temporary events and stop reacting to situations, which enables us to interact with others in a more mature way.

While practicing observation of our minds to improve our interactions with others, it is essential to distinguish observation from analysis. Many people are so accustomed to analysis that when they focus inwardly, rather than observing the mind they start analyzing its content. Analysis, a method of Western psychology, has proved valuable in studying the mind and emotional circuitry. But because it relies on thought it may encourage us to identify with the mind—and after we have processed an issue we are no closer to knowing our true selves. By contrast, in observation the mind is the subject, creating distance from our thoughts and emotions.

The following example clarifies this difference between analysis and observation. Sheela is having dinner with her husband Dev. The couple is enjoying a pleasant conversation; then their meal arrives, and they realize that the waitress has brought them the wrong order. Immediately, Dev's face flushes, his jaw tightens, and he raises his voice to the waitress. Sheela becomes nervous, feels an impulse to defend the waitress, but says nothing. The waitress apologizes for the mistake, assuring the couple she'll get the correct order as quickly as possible.

If Sheela analyzes her reaction to this incident, something like the following might occur: As soon as Dev raises his voice, Sheela feels anxiety and wonders why she is reacting so strongly. Immediately, she remembers experiencing similar anxiety as a child when her father would yell at her mother, and that at times she would defend her mother and her father would then focus his anger on her, which was frightening. She understands that's probably why she failed to stick up for the waitress. As she thinks about the interaction between her husband and the waitress, she comprehends why a seemingly minor incident might trigger such a strong reaction—and she realizes that this insight can be helpful in addressing her fear.

In this example, most of Sheela's energy goes into thinking. She ponders the situation, framing it in terms of cause and effect. The result of her thinking is a clear insight about a pattern in her relationship with her husband based on the memory of interactions between her mother and father long ago. The insight may be helpful in understanding her reaction to her husband's anger, but because her mental energy is engaged in analysis she remains strongly identified with her mind and her image of herself as a person driven by fear. The focus of Sheela's analysis is on fixing the problem, and she comes up with a strategy to do this: the next time she experiences anxiety, she will remind herself that she is no longer a helpless child but an adult with the resources to deal with her fear.

On the other hand, if Sheela practices observation the scene might look somewhat different: Sheela notices the waitress placing a dish with chicken on the table; she observes her husband's flushed face and clenched jaw, and hears him yelling at the waitress; she notices that her own heart is pounding, her mouth feels dry, and her stomach is churning. She remembers seeing her father get angry at her mother and jumping into the middle of the battle to defend her mother. She observes that she is thinking about a memory and returns her attention to the present moment. She hears the waitress apologize and sees Dev's face become more relaxed. She then observes her own body. As she focuses on the sensation in her chest, she feels the tightness begin to dissolve; her breathing starts to deepen, and she feels warmth in her stomach. Throughout this episode, Sheela focuses on watching, rather than thinking about, what is happening.

In reality, few people can observe their own minds quite so simply. Our minds churn out a bubbling stew of emotions, opinions, associations, plans, and random static—particularly when we're in the grip of our *vasanas*. A flash of anger at our partner arises, then a memory of a past injury surfaces; that memory triggers fifty more memories, along with a panicky sense that something is wrong and needs to be fixed immediately. Then maybe we remember to breathe and observe what's going on.

As we practice observation of our minds, we find good intentions are not enough. We are blind to our own lack of awareness, which is not surprising since the nature of unconsciousness is to be unaware. We are like the four

monks in a Hindu tale who took a vow of silence. They all
managed to refrain from speaking for half a day, but then
the first one blurted out, "I wonder what time it is."
The second one replied, "You just broke the vow of silence."
"No, stupid, you both broke it," the third monk said.
The last monk stood up and announced, "I am the only
one who remembered!"

Despite our chronic lack of consciousness, with per-
sistence we can cultivate awareness. As Sheela observes her
mind, she notices a pattern. It's not just Dev who triggers
her anxiety; she sees a number of different situations that
catalyze the same physiological sensations of anxiety—the
pounding heart, dry mouth, and churning stomach. As she
continues to observe, she gradually develops the ability to
sustain these sensations without thinking about them or
trying to push them away. She then begins to understand
that her anxiety is part of a deep, underlying *vasana* that
distorts her view of the world and prevents her from fully
enjoying life.

UNVEILING THE TRUE SELF

As Sheela continues observing her reactive patterns,
she feels less identified with anxiety, viewing it with more
detachment as a storm on the horizon that comes and goes
rather than as an essential attribute of her identity. This

detachment increases the more she disengages from her thoughts and emotions, no longer repressing them or even thinking about them.

The ability to observe as various mental and emotional states arise and dissipate requires an understanding and acceptance of their transitory nature. When we take our emotions and thoughts to be real and permanent, we are powerless to change our inner state. If Sheela defines herself as an anxious person who must be shielded from anger, she is at the mercy of the external world, which is full of expressions of anger. In an attempt to protect herself, she might embark on a campaign to reform her husband so that he never expresses anger; she might cut off her relationships with other people who express anger and avoid situations involving conflict. However, none of these actions is likely to improve the quality of her relationships or make her happy. And by trying to avoid situations where anger might arise she reinforces her anxiety, validating its power and thus strengthening her anxiety *vasana*.

At the same time, trying to suppress emotions and thoughts is equally counterproductive. Thoughts and emotions are a natural part of the flow of consciousness. Forcefully pushing them away creates tension, and though repression may work in the short term, eventually all repressed material will erupt in a torrent.

The longer Sheela persists in observing the rise and fall of thoughts and emotions without analyzing them or pushing them away, the more deeply she understands that she is neither the continually changing emotions nor the constant stream of thoughts flowing through her consciousness. Over years of observation, her reactions lose their power; she no longer feels afraid of her own anxiety; and gradually her *vasana* of anxiety diminishes. She can respond to Dev's anger in a more detached way. Her calm presence, which arises from her true self, will start to transform their relationship. And because when Dev gets angry she no longer reacts in the way he expects, eventually his anger also arises less often.

Like Sheela, we can learn to watch our critical thoughts about our partner arise: a hundred times, a thousand times, a million times. We just watch—without judging ourselves for our thoughts. We watch as we become indignant, thinking about how he *should* be. Slowly as we continue observing, we become quietly detached from our agendas. We allow the emotions to play without acting on them; and when they subside, we realize this seemingly powerful *vasana* is just one more mental projection.

The patient, steady quality of observing the mind contrasts markedly with the turbulence of the mind's contents. It's like a wise old grandmother who's seen it all watching the tantrum of her two-year-old grandson. No matter how dramatically the child wails, she lovingly watches, knowing that at any second his mood will shift.

It is easy to get entangled in thoughts—particularly the kind of obsessive thoughts generated by *vasanas*—instead of dealing with them objectively. But ruminating on our thoughts and emotions strengthens the ego and keeps us unaware of our true selves. However, when we practice observation, shifting our attention away from habitual inclinations, we gain a more objective perspective—the space of non-mind—which leads to peace. The Mandukya Upanishad describes this way of seeing:

> Whatever that is perceived in this world, movable or immovable, is nothing but the perceptions of the mind, is nothing but the mind. For plurality is not perceived when the mind is transcended.[1]

As this space of non-mind reveals itself, we find a new foundation for our actions. When we identify less with the fabricated "me," our true selves are no longer veiled by the mind's delusion and our decisions are guided not merely by our own desires but by whatever benefits the greater good. As we experience our true selves, we begin to relate to others with balance and joy regardless of the circumstances. Wisdom, clarity, compassion, and love—qualities inherent in our consciousness—then emerge, further diminishing the pull of our *vasanas*. Less enslaved by our past conditioning, we can love and appreciate the people in our lives for who they truly are.

EXERCISES

1. Sit comfortably, with spine, neck, and head aligned, in a crossed-legged position on a yoga mat or carpeted floor, or in a chair. Observe your in and out breath for a few seconds without attempting to change it. Now observe your thoughts as they arise; simply witness them, without becoming involved in them or judging them. Next move your attention from your thoughts to your spine, then bring it back to your breathing. Once again shift your attention from your thoughts to your spine then to your breathing. If you notice your mind becoming distracted, shift your focus back to observing your thoughts. Practice this form of internal observation for five to seven minutes once a day for a month, preferably in the same place at the same time.

2. After a month of practicing internal observation, observe how you react to other people and external situations. Practice this form of external observation once a week for six weeks.

3. After six weeks of practicing external observation, practice both internal and external observation for six months. Then notice any differences in the way you respond to yourself, others, and everyday situations. You will likely see subtle changes as you shift from participant to observer, no longer identifying with the content of your thoughts and emotions but simply watching them without disconnecting from other people.

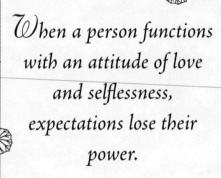

When a person functions
with an attitude of love
and selflessness,
expectations lose their
power.

4

The Path of Action
WORKING WITH RELATIONSHIPS IN DAILY LIFE

*HE WHO DOES ACTIONS, OFFERING THEM TO THE
SUPREME LORD, WITHOUT ATTACHMENT, IS NOT TAINTED
BY SIN, JUST AS A LOTUS LEAF REMAINS UNAFFECTED
BY THE WATER ON IT.*

—Bhagavad Gita

THE TRADITIONAL TERM IN VEDANTA for the path of action is "karma yoga." Known as the way of right action, karma yoga is a straightforward, practical technique that brings peace and happiness. The beauty of this path is that we can practice it wherever we are. Rather than retreating to a cave, monastery, or ashram, we can practice karma yoga in the midst of our endless desires, daily routines, and messy relationships. Because we're continually engaged in action with others—the dog, the computer, the dirty dishes in the sink, or our closest friend—karma yoga provides a way to work with relationships every day in any situation.

The word *karma* is derived from the root *kr*, which means to act. Although *karma* has many meanings, in the context of karma yoga it means a person's attitude toward actions and the results of those actions. To practice the path of action, we don't need to change our circumstances; instead, we change our attitude. We focus on benefiting others rather than serving ourselves. When we act without selfish desire, the power of existing *vasanas* becomes diminished. Martin Luther King's description of work captures the attitude of karma yoga: "If a person sweeps the streets for a living, he should sweep them as Michelangelo painted, as Beethoven composed music, as Shakespeare wrote his plays."[1]

Let's take a simple example: I need to wash the dishes. If I approach the sink with an attitude of resentment, seeing the dishes as one more act of drudgery to be endured before I finally get to have a cup of tea, I have already set up a conflict in my relationship with my work. As I start washing, my mind is dwelling on the many obstacles preventing me from fulfilling my desire. I encounter a plate crusted with dried egg even though I've asked my roommate many times to rinse the dishes before piling them in the sink. I may even rehash an argument with a friend, imagining what I could have said to her.

By contrast, if I'm practicing the path of action I view the pile of dirty dishes as part of that path. I approach dishwashing not as one more task to be stoically endured but as another way of devoting myself to whatever needs attention. When I act with this attitude, work becomes an expression of my true self. I work in a focused way, carefully washing each fork, each cup, the egg-encrusted plate, the bowl. Relationships with other people pose more challenges than relationships with dishes, but the practice is the same. We learn to see the grouchy, overworked bureaucrat who asks us to fill out five more forms as a human being worthy of our attention, respect, and consideration. We learn to observe our irritation as he hands us the pile of forms, take a deep breath, and remember our intention to act for the benefit of everyone.

Each day we encounter situations where we can refuse to reinforce our negative *vasanas*. And every time we choose to go against the grain of our conditioning we move closer to our true selves and create deeper, more authentic relationships.

TEMPERING THE POWER OF *VASANAS* IN RELATIONSHIPS

A man suffered from an irritable disposition and frequently exploded in fits of rage. Soon he had hurt most of his friends and family members, and people began to avoid him. Determined to conquer his *vasana* of anger, he retreated to a cave to meditate. Within days his mind felt calm, his entire body was at peace, and his irritability had dissipated.

Finally, after several years of meditation, he triumphantly returned to his hometown. As word of his return spread, a crowd of family and friends gathered to meet him.

"What did you learn?" his oldest friend asked.

"Well," he reflected, "the most important thing is that I have conquered my anger."

"Oh, come on," said the man's brother. "I know you. You must still have some anger."

"No, none. My anger is totally gone. In ten years, I haven't felt even a trace of anger," the man claimed.

"Really?" said another friend. "That's hard to believe about anyone—especially a hothead like you. I can't imagine you don't sometimes get angry."

"I already told you. My anger is gone. Do you need a sworn statement signed in blood?" the man asked.

"I can believe, maybe, that you're less angry than before, but to say you've totally conquered your anger—that's impossible," his oldest friend stated, shaking his head.

The man's face turned red, and he asserted, enraged, "My anger has completely vanished. I have no anger—none, none, none!"

Although meditation is an invaluable discipline that increases awareness of the true self, *vasanas*—with their deep, tenacious roots in the human psyche—don't necessarily disappear in the solitude of a cave or meditation room. They are created in interactions with the world—in relationships—and they are most effectively uprooted when we engage with other people while carrying our perspective from meditation. As we observe our *vasanas* in day-to-day interactions and refrain from acting on them, they begin to wear down.

In my own experience, I can feel quite loving in my meditation room, but the best opportunity to diminish the power of my *vasana* of anger comes when I am face-to-face with the person who annoys me most. Then I can consciously act in a way that goes against the grain of my conditioned reactions: rather than gritting my teeth or running from the encounter, I can take a deep breath and smile.

If I carefully observe my mind, both in meditation and in daily life, I notice how *vasanas* continually generate desires, which then dictate my actions. Desires seem endless. I want my morning coffee right away, but the room is cold. I turn up the heat and drink my coffee, but before finishing it I want a second cup. Now that the house has warmed, I notice my chair is a bit hard, and I wish it had a cushion; I move onto the couch. On and on, the mind spins out an endless stream of desires that propel us to act.

Although *vasanas* are usually buried deep in the unconscious as latent cravings, they express themselves in the conscious mind as desires, such as the desire for a drink, the desire for a new partner, or the urge to write a poem. Then the desires drive our actions: we order a shot of whiskey, flirt with a stranger, start to write.

We carry such desires into our relationships. Olga would like Pierre to spend more time with her. Then, finally, he takes a day off from work and she wants him to interact more with the kids. Pierre likes slender women and wishes Olga were thinner; she loses weight, and he thinks she looks great. Then he wonders why she so rarely expresses appreciation for all the things he does for her.

Desires in themselves are natural; it is the attitude behind them that determines whether they are wholesome, inconsequential, or damaging. Wholesome desires can contribute to personal happiness and benefit society. People like Nelson Mandela and Aung San Suu Kyi have demonstrated how a strong desire to help others can improve the lives of millions of people. Many other desires—like the wish for a softer chair—are fairly inconsequential. Still others can have devastating and lasting effects. A recent example is the greed leading to the 2008 financial crisis in the United States. By focusing on their selfish ambitions, executives overlooked the welfare of their institutions and the individuals who trusted them to protect their interests, affecting the lives of millions of people.

HARNESSING THE POWER OF FREE WILL

Vedanta teaches a method for weakening the grip of *vasanas* by harnessing the power of free will. Since *vasanas* drive our actions, each choice about how to act can either loosen or strengthen the grip of negative *vasanas*. Too often we respond automatically—without considering the effects of our choices—and in doing so we deepen the imprint of habitual patterns. Through meditation and observation, however, we bring unconscious desires to consciousness and understand how acting on them affects other people. That is when we can harness the power of free will and choose to act more consciously.

To begin using free will to make more conscious choices about our actions, we first need to become more aware of the conditions under which we choose our actions. From the second we wake up in the morning until we go to bed at night, we make choices about how to act—and the attitude we bring to those actions. In my experience, when the alarm rings I decide whether to jump out of bed or sink back into the covers for a few more minutes. I choose whether to smile at my neighbor—even though I'm feeling grumpy—or to look down at the sidewalk as I pass, pretending not to notice her. I can decide to take the time to help my co-worker resolve his concerns about his project or I can focus on my own project. When I return home feeling tired from a long, difficult day, I can mindlessly snap at my partner or I can let him know I need a few minutes to unwind before talking.

By choosing how to respond rather than automatically reacting, we can conserve energy, avoid conflict, and avert minor crises. For example, I'm already late for work and on my way out of the house when I remember I left an important folder on the desk. I open the front door and hear my mother yelling that we're out of coffee and I should go get some right away; then my daughter announces the toilet is overflowing all over the bathroom floor. As I run back into the house, the cat saunters in with a half-dead bird in her mouth. At that moment, I can react with anger or panic, or, remembering I'm free to respond as I wish, I can simply breathe and calm my mind, reflect on the situation, and rationally decide which issue to address first. I don't have to react from my conditioned patterns by arguing with my mother about whether running out of coffee constitutes a genuine emergency or make a heroic but futile effort to save an already-doomed bird. Instead, I can opt to use my energy effectively by grabbing the mop and heading for the bathroom to deal with the flood.

Other animals have little choice but to act on desires. A cat sees a bird, it pounces; a dog tracks a ball through the air and races after it. Humans, however, can make conscious, considered decisions, not only about how to act but also about the attitude driving those actions. As Swami Chinmayananda wrote, "Though our activities appear to be defined by our tendencies, man has the unique capacity, which is denied to other living creatures, to exercise his self-effort in choosing his actions. By a persistent and prolonged application of this great faculty, every human being can erase his inherent tendencies and reach the pinnacle of perfection."[2]

In harnessing the power of free will to make wise choices and the inspiration of selfless love to work for the benefit of others, we deepen our connections with others. Every time our actions are motivated by egocentric desire, we reinforce negative *vasanas*; on the other hand, each time we act selflessly we wear down those same patterns. If we choose to work for the welfare of other people and dedicate our actions to the greater good, negative *vasanas* begin to weaken and the mind becomes more peaceful. As the obscurations of *vasanas* clear, we can express our true selves more freely and also see other people as embodiments of divine essence.

DIMINISHING ATTACHMENT AND
EXPECTATIONS IN RELATIONSHIPS

When a person's actions are motivated by a desire for reward or recognition, negative *vasanas* are reinforced. In contrast, selfless actions weaken the grip of *vasanas*, reduce stress, and help unveil the true self. The Bhagavad Gita, in chapter 3, verse 7, summarizes this path: "But, whosoever, controlling the senses by the mind, O Arjuna, engages his organs of action in karma-yoga without attachment, he excels."[3]

Work done with a strong attachment to a particular outcome often causes stress and anxiety. An actor obsessed by a desire to deliver an impressive performance may concentrate so much on the audience's response that his self-consciousness undermines his performance. On the other hand, an actor focused on becoming his character, without attachment to presenting a brilliant performance, may paradoxically perform brilliantly.

When a person's actions are motivated only by selfish desires, his work becomes uninspiring labor. However, the work of someone expressing his true self will benefit others.

The path of action asks us to give up expectations and surrender selflessly to whatever needs to be done in the moment. A story about the Duke of Norfolk illustrates the selfless, spontaneous action of someone skilled in the path of action. Although the Duke of Norfolk was a powerful ruler and lived in a lavish castle, he was unattached to his position and selflessly served his people without expectations. One day an Irish immigrant who had been hired as a servant for the duke arrived at the railroad station with a very large and heavy suitcase. Because the duke's castle was more than a mile from the station, she needed to hire a porter to carry her luggage. But the only money she had was a shilling, and no one in the crowd of porters looking for work would carry her monstrous bag for so little money.

Luckily the duke himself happened to be at the station observing the scene, dressed in plain clothes so no one recognized him. When he saw the girl's dilemma, he immediately picked up her suitcase, carried it all the way to the castle, and courteously accepted the shilling as payment. Not until the following day, when the girl began her job, did she realize the identity of the helpful porter. The duke, in acting selflessly and spontaneously, without expectations, had accomplished this feat with ease.

Often we aren't aware of the expectations we bring to relationships. But in observing our minds over time we can see how we project our desires and expectations onto others during our interactions with them. The mail carrier should deliver the mail by 2:00 pm; our niece should marry a well-educated man; when we're having a crisis, our friends should drop what they're doing to listen to us; on our birthday, our partners should bring us flowers; our co-workers should keep us informed about the status of their projects.

The first step in giving up expectations to weaken the grip of *vasanas* is to simply acknowledge their existence. Often we think things should go a certain way; then, when our expectations aren't met, we feel life is unfair and are blind to the cause of our distress. People tend to confuse reality, or how the world is, with their expectations of how it should be. The sun will rise in the east and set in the west—this is reality. The mail will arrive by 2:00 pm—this is my expectation; but of course, if the mail carrier is sick or gets stuck in traffic my expectation won't be met. Knowing that my expectation is motivated by personal desire rather than a moral precept or a law of physics, I might feel less grouchy when the mail doesn't show up on schedule.

The following scenario illustrates the choices we can make in working with expectations. Suzanne just spent eight long hours taking care of young children and can't wait for her husband Claude to get home so she can have a conversation with someone who speaks in full sentences. She's cleaned up the spilled juice and cookie crumbs, put away the toys, cooked a special dinner, set flowers on the table, and put on a new dress. Claude arrives home an hour

late, drenched from having changed a flat tire in a torren-
tial rainstorm—one of many problems in his crisis-filled
day. He's relieved to be home, ready for a simple dinner and
an evening on the couch in front of the TV. Above all, he's
craving some time alone.

What happens next depends on the couple's awareness,
ability to let go of expectations, and their love for each
other. Suzanne and Claude could both insist on immediately
getting their needs met and watch the evening degenerate
into a series of arguments accompanied by hurt, anger, and
bitterness. But luckily they are familiar with their *vasanas*
and choose not to let them motivate their actions. Suzanne
knows her tendency to become hurt and irritable when her
expectations are dashed; Claude knows that if he's feeling
pressured he can quickly wreck an evening with his biting
criticism. Consequently, both understand the value of letting
go of their personal desires and acting from love and concern
for each other.

As a result, the following scenario gradually unfolds.
Claude walks in the door dripping muddy water on the
newly vacuumed rug and, complaining about the flat tire
and his disastrous day, staggers up to the bedroom to change
out of his wet clothes. Suzanne feels a sense of foreboding
and starts to observe her reactions. She notices she's feeling
hurt at the curtness of Claude's greeting; soon her hurt is

overshadowed by the bleak realization that the cozy evening she's expecting isn't going to happen. She observes she's feeling annoyed and frustrated, and she understands these familiar emotions as warning signs reminding her that she needs to look at the situation from a wider perspective. She shifts her attention to Claude, trying to understand what his day has been like and how he's feeling. She imagines what it's like to kneel on the road in the middle of traffic and be drenched with rain while tightening lug nuts. As she tunes in to Claude's experience, she realizes he's probably exhausted and needs time to rest. He's also probably hungry but not up for a prolonged dinner.

Once Claude has changed out of his wet clothes, he sits on the bed and breathes deeply. His body relaxes enough to become aware of what just happened. He realizes he missed something in the living room: the table with flowers and the best dishes, his wife wearing a dress. He realizes she's been cooped up all day taking care of kids and wants an intimate evening together, while all he can think about is a cold beer on the couch in front of the TV. He knows he needs to talk to her before they end up in a war of conflicting desires.

Claude and Suzanne have made a commitment to work for the overall good of their marriage. They've learned that when their expectations clash each needs to momentarily

shift their focus from their own point of view and look at
the situation through the other's eyes. Then they need to
consider a third perspective: the health and growth of their
marriage.

Five minutes later they discuss the situation and work
out a plan. They'll have a quick dinner together and catch
up; after dinner, Claude will watch TV while Suzanne visits
a friend; tomorrow evening they'll go out to their favorite
restaurant and celebrate their relationship.

When expectations collide in relationships, *vasanas*
come to the surface. Often one person will judge the other
for the patterns they're exhibiting. Claude could easily dis-
miss Suzanne's desire for connection as "needy," or Suzanne
could judge Claude's desire for time alone as "self-absorbed."
Equally common is the tendency to judge ourselves for the
patterns we're exhibiting, feeling we shouldn't want what
we want. The wisest option when patterns arise is to realize
we all suffer from conditioning and we all need to be gentle
with ourselves and others. Claude and Suzanne provide a
useful example of how to do this. Their straightforward
acceptance of both their own and their partner's desires
allows them to work with their patterns in an honest and
compassionate way.

Sometimes I'm asked to give a speech at weddings, and
I've been told that my "low expectation" speech has been

getting a lot of buzz. After I congratulate the bride and groom and both their families, I remind them that marriage is mainly about love and support. If two people start their journey with minimal and realistic expectations, chances are they will be happier sooner and longer.

If we have too many expectations of our partner, we will inevitably be disappointed. Everyone has weaknesses, and, given the many demands of everyday life, even the most well-meaning partner falls short of the other's expectations. But when we enter a relationship with realistic expectations, even a small caring action from our partner makes us happy.

Of course, some expectations are necessary. Basic moral principles—honesty, integrity, and fidelity—form the foundation of healthy relationships. But if we expect a lot in the beginning, once the honeymoon is over and the laundry starts piling up we'll end up frustrated.

Love is a key ingredient in diminishing expectations. When a person functions with an attitude of love and selflessness, expectations lose their power. Weaknesses, limitations, and defilements of *vasanas* start to slowly fall away. When selfless service becomes a habit, a sense of peace develops. As the mind calms, stress diminishes, thought becomes clearer, and the heart opens, the play of relationships becomes richer and more meaningful.

The Sufi poet Rumi summed it up:

Let the beauty
Of what you love
Be what you do.
There are a thousand ways to bow and kiss the earth.[4]

EXERCISES

1. Choose a person you don't know well. Randomly do something for them without any kind of expectation. Notice how you feel about the action.

2. Choose one day a week in which to be conscious of your desires. During that day, notice your reactions to others regarding those desires. How do you feel if they are fulfilled? If they are not fulfilled? How does a desire pull you out of the present moment by causing you to focus on the past or future? How can you work with the desire in the present moment? Write down your findings.

3. Select three people to whom you are attached. Consider how you can progress with these relationships by becoming more loving and less attached. Next identify three expectations you have of these people, one per person. Now close your eyes and see the attachments perish one by one. Notice what you feel. Write down your feelings.

When we devote our time and attention to others, we serve ourselves as well, thereby increasing our capacity for love and happiness.

5

The Path of Love and Devotion
CULTIVATING SELFLESSNESS IN RELATIONSHIPS

[THE] TRUTH EXISTING EVER IN THE HEART ALONE
IS TO BE KNOWN; INDEED, THERE IS NOTHING
WHATSOEVER TO BE KNOWN BEYOND THIS.

—Svetasvatara Upanishad

THE HUMAN CAPACITY FOR SELFLESS LOVE can be brought forward to enrich our relationships. Love that is directed toward the universal self is called *bhakti*, or devotion. The Sanskrit word *bhakti* comes from the root *bhaj*, which means to adore or worship God. The practice of devotion centers on a personal relationship to the divine or the true self. Depending on the person's particular inclination, she may focus on a deity, a guru, God, or a symbol of the divine. Or she may connect with a formless manifestation, focusing on spirit, the true self, the transcendent, or the source of life. Regardless of the particular practice, the key is to focus on something that inspires deep love.

A person who taps into the source of love naturally develops a sense of trust in a benevolent, wise universe. When she is able to see that power as the basis of all life and recognize it in everyone, her relationships take on new meaning. She interacts with the world with love and uses her energy in a way that expresses her true self.

Although the practice of love and devotion is very desirable, selfless love and devotion are not easy to attain. Letting go of expectations is difficult; we are deeply conditioned to believe we are separate, competing individuals; we have no magic pill to instantly eradicate our negative *vasanas* deriving from our egocentric selves; we must gain awareness to see our own and other people's true selves; and many of us grow up in cultures that value competition over cooperation, success and wealth over kindness and generosity.

The following story compares the outcomes of actions inspired by selfless love and devotion with actions motivated by desires of the ego-centered self. Once there was a wealthy woman who employed a cook, a driver, and a gardener. She lived alone and gave most of her money to charity, but she paid her own employees a paltry wage, somehow not seeing them as worthy of her generosity. And she made certain she got her money's worth for the little she did pay them, working them hard and often treating them harshly. Since she gave so much money to good causes, she thought of herself as a pious and extremely generous person, and she expected that her generosity would eventually be rewarded.

In spite of the way the woman treated them, her employees, steeped in their village tradition, saw her for who she was: beneath the surface of her grouchy disposition, they saw a frightened, lonely old woman, and beneath that they saw the beauty of the true self that connects us all. Because they recognized her for who she truly was, they worked hard, serving her with devotion.

One day, after many years, the cook died. Shortly afterward the driver and the gardener died, and soon after that the woman herself died. When the woman reached the pearly gates of heaven, a beautiful limousine was waiting to take her to her new abode. As the chauffeur drove her down the streets of paradise, she saw a luxurious house.

"Is that mine?" she asked.

"No, madam," the driver answered. "That belongs to your gardener." The woman started getting excited. *If my gardener has such a beautiful house, mine must be really fabulous,* she thought. Very soon they came to a magnificent villa.

"Is that mine?" she asked again.

"No, madam," the chauffeur answered. "That belongs to your driver." The woman felt ecstatic, imagining the splendid residence awaiting her. Pretty soon she saw a castle.

Before she could even ask, the driver said, "This belongs to your cook, who fed you day and night." At that point, the woman gave up trying to visualize what her own dwelling would be like.

Suddenly the limousine turned onto a dirt road and entered a slum area.

"Driver, I think you just made a wrong turn," the woman said abruptly.

"No, madam, there is no mistake. Your home is here on the right," he said, pointing to a simple one-room hut.

"How can that be!" the woman exclaimed.

"Madam, here we construct the accommodations from the materials you left us during your life. Your cook, your driver, and your gardener served you selflessly, with love, expecting nothing in return. They left materials of the highest quality. You, on the other hand, also performed good deeds, but you acted with pride and with the expectation of reward. Meanwhile, you didn't treat your employees kindly. The construction materials you left just weren't that good."

In this story, the highest-quality construction material is love. The cook, driver, and gardener had opened their hearts to see the inner essence of their cranky employer. Because they recognized her true self, they had loved her for who she really was.

CULTIVATING SELFLESSNESS

In spite of pervasive self-centeredness, people have an enormous capacity for love, which, if cultivated, can override selfishness. Every day we can find examples of spontaneous love and kindness: a two-year-old child races over to comfort a crying baby; a stranger stops to help a man whose car has broken down on the freeway; a woman cancels her plans for the day so she can assist a neighbor who's injured her back; a father stays up all night with a sick child so his wife can get some sleep. Such common acts of selflessness rarely make the nightly news, where reports of conflict and violence dominate the airwaves and assault our consciousness.

More dramatic examples of selflessness also occur frequently: in the midst of winter, a man dives into an icy river to save someone he's never met; a mother works for twenty years in a textile factory so her daughter can get an education; a brother donates a kidney to save his sister's life. Such selfless behavior arises in individuals who feel intimate connections with others as a result of having directed love toward themselves. This practice of devotion in relationships implies seeing other people as expressions of the divine, universal self and relating to them accordingly with love.

The idea of offering selfless devotion to others can seem frightening. We wonder whether it will set us up for disillusionment and whether people will see us as naive fools, blind to the reality of human nature, and take advantage of us. To some people, the term "selfless devotion" may sound sentimental and conjure up images of a self-effacing martyr slaving away for others while feeling resentful and unappreciated.

Actually, selflessness is far less frightening than selfishness. If we were truly able to see the amount of suffering caused by people's self-centered perspectives, we would be horrified. Wars, poverty, greed, abuse, environmental destruction—all are rooted in our pervasive, often unconscious self-absorption. When devotion to others flows from our true selves and awareness of the divine essence of others, it is not grudging self-sacrifice but rather an expression of joy. St. Bernard tells us, "Love seeks no cause beyond itself and no fruit; it is its own fruit, its own enjoyment. I love because I love; I love in order that I may love."[1]

The following scenario illustrates how love can be cultivated in relationships when devotion flows from the true self and acknowledgment of the divine essence of others, ultimately transforming the relationship. Mario was married to Cecilia, a gorgeous, intelligent, sharp-tongued woman who delighted in making fun of people, including Mario. When the couple went out with their friends, Cecilia loved to tell stories that made Mario look like an idiot. At home she was even blunter, pointing out every flaw in his behavior.

During the first few years of their marriage, Mario was so infatuated with Cecilia's beauty and intelligence that he overlooked the way she ridiculed him. But over time her put-downs became less subtle, and he felt increasingly angry at her. When Mario's Vedanta teacher suggested he try to generate love for his wife by seeing her as an embodiment of the divine, he was appalled. The idea of cultivating love for someone who didn't respect him seemed self-destructive. He wondered why he should reward her behavior with love, how he could envision a shrew like his wife as an embodiment of the divine, and even if he could, why it wouldn't further fuel her abuse.

Finally, as the marriage continued to deteriorate, Mario, in desperation, attempted the practice. He tried hard to generate love, but he found it impossible; instead, he experienced a range of unpleasant emotions: resentment, fear, anger, and confusion. He realized that before he could truly love anyone else he needed to find the source of love within himself. As he persisted with his practice, he began to feel compassion for himself. He saw how much he had suffered in his marriage—and he also realized he had been partly responsible for it by appeasing his wife, avoiding conflict with her, and allowing her to dump on him.

Over time Mario increasingly felt the sacredness of his own being and a connection with a spiritual feeling he couldn't explain. As this feeling deepened, he felt greater respect for himself. Instead of becoming a doormat for his wife's abuse, he had less tolerance for her behavior. In the past, he had pretended Cecilia's ridicule didn't bother him; then when that strategy wore thin, he would lash out at her. Now, neither ignoring her behavior nor berating her for it seemed appropriate.

The next time Cecilia started to make of fun of him he stopped her immediately, calmly but firmly telling her how he felt. At first, she seemed surprised, but she did stop. A few days later when she again started to deride him, Mario flatly asked her to stop. After Mario used this approach for a while, Cecilia's attacks became less frequent and eventually halted completely.

In turn, as his wife started treating him with more respect Mario felt less resentful. When he had first practiced devotion, no matter how he tried he was unable to see Cecilia as an embodiment of the divine. But as he connected more deeply with his own divine essence he found an abundance of love and realized love is a state of consciousness

that sees everyone as worthy of respect and devoted attention—even Cecilia.

Eventually, with practice Mario was able to reconnect
with the love he had felt for Cecilia in the early days of their
marriage, only now that love felt even deeper and more sta-
ble. When he looked at his wife, he saw a beautiful, complex being with a tenderness about her he had never before
noticed.

Beneath Cecilia's sharp-edged veneer was a woman
terrified of being hurt, who had learned to use her wit
to protect her from feeling vulnerable; her strategy was
to hurt others before they had a chance to hurt her. But
lately she could feel the authenticity and depth of Mario's
love, and she began to experience a foundation of safety
in her marriage. Consequently, instead of defending herself so often from some imagined threat, she became less
guarded with her husband. As her trust increased, she
was able to express her fear of being hurt. As a result, the
tone of their relationship shifted to one of mutual love,
honesty, and respect.

Vedanta doesn't ask anyone to be a doormat for other
people's aggression. The practice of devotion doesn't require
us to meekly allow others to step on us. But it does ask
us to see everything and everyone, including ourselves, as
an embodiment of the divine. And as an embodiment of

the divine we all deserve to be treated with respect and devotion.

People often falsely think of selfless devotion as a form of self-sacrifice. They believe that giving their time and attention to others means giving up a part of themselves. But in reality, the opposite is true. In moving away from identification with the ego-centered self, we are no longer enslaved by our *vasanas*, at which point we open to deeper energies, and devotion arises naturally. We begin to experience the infinite riches of our true selves—love, wisdom, wonder, confidence. Having given up self-preoccupation and suffering, we can move into a space of joy. When we devote our time and attention to others, we serve ourselves as well, thereby increasing our capacity for love and happiness. Instead of holding back out of fear, we might follow Rumi's advice:

> Gamble everything for love.
> Half-heartedness doesn't reach into majesty—
> You set out to find God,
> but then keep stopping for long periods at
> mean-spirited roadhouses.
> Dive in the ocean,
> leave and let the sea be you.[2]

THE NET OF INDRA: A WEB OF
INTERDEPENDENCE

The Avatamsaka Sutra, a Buddhist text, presents a
beautiful image that can illustrate the principles underlying both the practice of devotion and the path of action.
When the god Indra created the universe, he made it as an
infinite web with a knot at each node of the net. From every
knot, he hung a shimmering multifaceted jewel, and since
the web was infinite the number of these glittering jewels
was also infinite. When someone looks into just one of the
jewels, he sees reflected all the other jewels in the universe,
shimmering in a dazzling display. Everything that exists, or
has ever existed, is a jewel in Indra's net—and within each
of those jewels the entire radiant universe shines forth.

Each of us is a jewel in that infinite net, but because of
our limited self-centered perspective and the veil of delusions created by our *vasanas* we narrowly focus on the knot
rather than the jewel and don't even see who we are. The
practice of devotion teaches us to focus on the beauty of
the jewels. When we look into the jewel of our being, we
see reflected there the beauty of all other jewels: the jewel
of a pine tree, the jewel of an old woman on the street, the
jewel of a tiny purple flower peeking up from a crack in

the sidewalk. Thus the practice of devotion extends to all beings and life-forms, not just to the people we decide are important. All our lives are supported by this web made up of the billions of beings and life-forms in this vast universe.

Seeing the world in this way awakens a deep sense of the sacredness of life. Each movement of the web reverberates in all directions. Thus, as jewels in this interconnected web, our actions affect everything else. Not only are we responsible for our actions, but our actions have the power to affect the whole fabric of life. This understanding inspires love and devotion. And because the love we feel guides our actions in a way that maintains the integrity of Indra's net, love becomes the foundation for all our relationships.

EXERCISES

1. Chant aaaaaaaaaa. While chanting, consciously direct the energy from your head into your heart space. Do this a few times until you feel the energy shifting into your heart center.

2. Think of someone with whom you have a potentially close relationship despite some ongoing conflict. Then envision the person as an embodiment of the divine and consider how this view changes your opinions about the individual's actions and attitudes. Repeat this process when a conflict arises while interacting with the person.

3. During daily activities, notice acts of spontaneous love
    and kindness by others you encounter. Then perform
    one yourself.

*All our relationships—
with their ups and downs
and opportunities for
authentic connection—can
be used as practice that
transforms consciousness.*

6

The Path of Relationship
LOVE AND COMMITMENT

COMMITMENT IS AN ACT, NOT A WORD.

—Jean-Paul Sartre

W<small>E HAVE CONSIDERED</small> how the separate Vedanta practices of meditation, mantra, chanting, observation, selfless action, and devotion can diminish the power of *vasanas* so we can uncover our true selves and create deeper, more loving relationships. But gaining awareness of how these various practices work together in connection with relationships can not only further enhance our relationships but also help us see that relationships can be a practice that provides opportunities for personal transformation. For example, in a conflict with a friend, I use several different techniques: as I attempt to discuss the conflict with him, I observe my reactive patterns; then I take a break to chant my mantra and meditate to calm my mind; as I reengage in conversation and listen to him, I continue to observe my reactions and also generate love to help me stay centered.

When we begin studying Vedanta—which presents us with a range of practice suited for different temperaments and situations—we work on each practice separately. Only later do we integrate them, a process similar to learning a new language when we memorize vocabulary and grammatical structures before eventually integrating the different elements by engaging in conversations. Interestingly, as we begin integrating various Vedanta practices the relationships themselves become a powerful and challenging form of practice.

RELATIONSHIP AS PRACTICE

All our relationships—with their ups and downs and opportunities for authentic connection—can be used as practice that transforms consciousness. Because we spend most of our lives interacting with the world, once we understand that relationships can be an ongoing practice we can use them as endless opportunities for transformation.

A primary way relationships help us attain freedom from the grip of our *vasanas* is by making us aware of them. Because the mirror of relationships shows us emotions we would rather keep suppressed—anger, fear, grasping, vulnerability, and jealousy—it helps us see how these emotions trigger reactive patterns.

Often other people reveal to us qualities we hide from ourselves. When we run into difficulties with another person, it's therefore revealing to ask ourselves: *What does he or she show me about myself?* As Confucius instructed, "When we see men of contrary character, we should turn inward and examine ourselves."[1] If we honestly observe our reactions in relationships, we become familiar with our negative *vasanas* and understand how we keep ourselves stuck in the same reactive cycles. Relationships challenge us to question such reactive patterns so we can interact with greater awareness, as illustrated by the following story.

Robert was an insurance agent who grew up with a dominating, violent father who flew into a rage whenever Robert did anything his father didn't like. At age fifty-two, Robert constantly found himself embroiled in conflicts with other people. For years he blamed everyone else for his problems. "The world is full of jerks trying to take advantage of you. If you don't stand up to them, they'll walk all over you," he explained to anyone who would listen. When his third wife divorced him, he finally reached a crisis point and began seeing a counselor.

Robert's counselor encouraged him to examine the feelings beneath his anger, and after several months of raging at the counselor Robert began to notice the fear his anger masked. Without the armor of anger to protect him, he felt terrified—even in the safe space of the counselor's office. Gradually, he learned to stay present with his emotions, just observing them without trying to change anything. As his capacity to tolerate his own feelings deepened, he discovered a reservoir of tremendous sadness beneath both the anger and the fear. At last he was able to cry, expressing his grief for the small child who had lived in fear of doing the wrong thing— and for the fifty-two-year-old man who was unable to love.

Next Robert's counselor asked him to look at how his anger functioned as he interacted with people throughout the day. The following morning Robert observed himself snarling at a neighbor who had parked too close to his driveway. Then he noticed his irritation when a waitress in his neighborhood coffee shop put too much milk in his latte. At work when his ex-wife called him in the middle of the day, he lost his temper and yelled at his secretary, who had forgotten to fax some documents.

Each day he watched how his *vasana* of anger repeatedly arose, as if his father's hypercritical voice inhabited Robert, driving him to control everyone in his life. Once Robert fully understood his own conditioning as the source of his anger, he could drop his self-righteous indignation, observe how his anger functioned, and become aware of the fear underlying it. After months of observation, he finally realized he no longer needed to carry these emotions and had the power to change how he related to people.

One morning Robert managed to say hello to his neighbor in a pleasant way. Next he smiled at the waitress at the coffee shop, thanking her when she handed him his coffee, resulting in improved service thereafter. Several months later he made it through an entire conversation with his ex without raising his voice. In time he even began to feel affection for some of the people he previously had written off as "jerks." Robert still had work ahead of him, but with his increased awareness about relationships he found that interactions with other people were providing him with the information he needed to transform himself.

The practice of relationship asks us to move past automatic reactions and grow toward greater freedom in all aspects of our lives. Such practice means interacting with awareness and observing how we actually behave with others rather than how we would like to think we behave. In my own experience, I know that relationships can be hard. People don't act the way I want them to; they disappoint me, bore me, and activate the anger I don't want to experience since I like to think of myself as a nice person. I notice how many of the little annoyances in relationships—disappointment, boredom, and anger—reflect my inner states.

I see how driven I am by my likes and dislikes, which set me up for disappointment when others don't act the way I want them to, which occurs often. My boredom shows me the self-centeredness blocking me from being fully present with others. My anger, I realize, isn't *caused* by anyone else; it's already there beneath the surface of my pleasant smile, like hot lava waiting to spill forth.

Fortunately, relationships also reveal positive qualities. Over time we become more aware of our genuine concern for the people in our lives. Love, compassion, and kindness arise spontaneously. The more we can detach from our negative *vasanas*, the more we experience genuine caring and intimate connection to others. Increasingly, we find moments when, unexpectedly, the warmth of unconditional love radiates from deep within us. As we awaken more fully to that love, we experience a goodness within ourselves and an increased appreciation for the people we encounter.

THE FOUNDATION OF RELATIONSHIP

At the heart of Vedanta lies the understanding that in my essence I am no different from you. Jesus put the same idea in more concrete language: "Love your neighbor as yourself" (Mark 12:31). This understanding of deep interconnection provides the crucial starting point for any relationship. We can attend relationship seminars, read books, memorize communication techniques, and learn to say exactly the right thing; but if our underlying motivation for improving relationship skills is to manipulate people for our own self-interest our relationships still rest on a shaky foundation of "us versus them," a self-serving orientation that at some level we communicate despite our best efforts not to. If, on the other hand, we feel genuinely concerned about other people, even when our words are less than perfect, we will communicate our love.

The love we experience for others prepares the ground for commitment in relationships. When we see other people as ourselves, we feel intimately connected to them, naturally care about their well-being, put time and energy into the relationships, and feel committed to supporting them. Pablo Neruda, in a love sonnet, beautifully expressed this experience of deep connection:

> I love you without knowing how, or when, or from where,
> I love you simply, without problems or pride:
> I love you in this way because I don't know any other
>   way of loving
> but this, in which there is no I or you,
> so intimate that your hand upon my chest is my hand,
> so intimate that when I fall asleep it is your eyes that
>   close.[2]

When we experience depth of connection in a relationship, commitment and desire to support the other person
arises naturally. But when love is difficult—as it often is—a
consciously willed commitment can sustain us through the
challenging times.

Although writings of religious traditions from a variety
of cultures reflect the joys and challenges of committed love,
modern global culture is so fixated on novelty and change
that the idea of commitment can seem outdated. We're conditioned to value what is easy and to look for something newer,
better, and more exciting—attitudes that affect the way we
view our relationships. In a search for ever more happiness,
we discard computers, cars, employees, friends, husbands,
and wives, replacing them with newer models we believe will
do the job better. People have become like commodities that
we evaluate in terms of how well they meet our needs rather
than appreciating them for who they are.

Without a sense of commitment, we can easily decide
the ongoing challenges of relationships are too hard and
walk away. Our partner is too difficult; the way he chews
his food is annoying; he smokes; he doesn't share our taste
in movies; he doesn't appreciate us enough—we need to
trade him in for a new model. Commitment to relationships means we don't get to blame our partner, slam the
door, and run off to find someone new. We stay in the situ-

ation, observing our reactions, but rather than allowing our negative *vasanas* to dictate our actions, we begin relating from a space of love and awareness.

Commitment provides the soil for cultivating acceptance, one of the most essential—and often forgotten—elements in relationships. When we are committed to a relationship, we accept our partner for who they are and don't try to change them to fit our preferences. We realize their path may be different from ours, and what's right for us isn't necessarily right for them. Relationships aren't about trying to fix other people, to make them into who we want them to be. Rather they give us opportunities to express our love by respecting our partner and supporting them on their path. This doesn't mean that if someone is acting in a destructive way we accept it. But it does mean we remember our way of doing things isn't necessarily right for everyone else. In a broader sense, such acceptance in relationships leads to tolerance of others in different cultures, a foundation for decreasing global conflict.

By committing to relationships and increasing our capacity for acceptance, we swim against the current of consumer culture, and, even more challenging, we go against our own self-centered tendencies. People aren't products who exist for convenience or entertainment. All of us embody the essence of the divine but, to one degree or another, have forgotten this. We need each other so we can wake up to the love and joy that is our birthright. Commitment provides a container for this awakening.

The mirror of relationships thus allows us to discover the joy that results when we commit to love from the depth of our hearts. The Sufi poet Hafiz, in his poem "The Gift," poignantly described this state of selfless commitment:

> Our union is like this:
> You feel cold
> So I reach for a blanket to cover
> Our shivering feet.
>
> A hunger comes into your body
> So I run to my garden
> And start digging potatoes.
>
> You ask for a few words of comfort and guidance,
> I quickly kneel at your side offering you
> This whole book—as a gift.
>
> You ache with loneliness one night
> So much you weep.

And I say,
Here's a rope,
Tie it around me,

Hafiz
Will be your companion
For life.[3]

EXERCISES

1. Write the names of three people with whom you have a close personal relationship and three people who are professional associates. On a scale of 1 to 10 (with 10 being the highest), rate your current level of commitment toward each of them.

2. Write the names of three old friends or relatives and three acquaintances you have not known very long. Next write one word that describes your feelings toward them, either positive or negative. Finally, describe one way you could improve your relationship with each individual.

PART THREE

The Practice of Relationships

When we let go of the judgments that reinforce our sense of separateness, we open to the source of empathy—our interconnection with others.

7

Engaging in Open Listening

So when you are listening to somebody
completely, attentively, then you are listening
not only to the words but also to the feeling
of what is being conveyed, to the whole of it,
not just part of it.

—Jiddu Krishnamurti

WHEN CALVIN COOLIDGE was president of the United States, he saw dozens of people each day, most of whom had complaints of one kind or another. One day a visiting governor told the president that he didn't understand how he was able to meet so many people in the space of a few hours.

"Why, you are finished with all your visitors by dinnertime," said the governor, "while I am often in my office till midnight."

"Yes," said Coolidge, "that's because you talk."

THE VALUE OF LISTENING

Many people view communication as a means to an end—a set of verbal techniques to master so they can get their needs met. From this perspective, communication is successful when other people agree with our point of view and do what we want them to. In the short term, we may get our way; but over time if communication is aimed at manipulation, we undermine the basis of an authentic relationship. This situation is exemplified by the relationship in the following scenario.

Kara was a sensitive, gentle woman who thought of herself as a highly spiritual person. A devoted Vedanta student, she practiced meditation, chanted mantras, and practiced bhakti yoga. Over the years of her marriage to Raj, her spiritual practices had increasingly become the central focus of her life. She had even adopted a vegetarian diet. These days she was often busy organizing events at the spiritual center where she studied.

Raj was a practical, sociable, tough-minded business-man. He had worked his way up in a small electronics company that, under his leadership, had become highly successful. Now, serving as senior manager, he was rarely home. During the week, business occupied his every moment; on weekends he liked to go to the gym or hang out with his friends.

Both Raj and Kara were unhappy with their relationship. When Raj first met Kara, she had just discovered her spiritual practice, which, at the time, Raj had believed was a passing novelty. However, lately it seemed she had become obsessed with it. She was up at sunrise, lighting incense and chanting her mantras. She talked about little except her spiritual teacher, whom she quoted constantly, along with incoherent phrases from ancient religious texts. Still, Raj saw how important her spiritual life was to her, so he tried to support her in her practice, but he found this difficult. Kara wouldn't leave him alone; she wanted to convert him, and lectured him every chance she got, telling him how he should live and urging him to attend talks at her spiritual center.

Kara felt her marriage was a total failure. She yearned for a spiritual connection with Raj—a connection of mutual devotion and love. But all he seemed to care about were spreadsheets, computers, and watching sports with his friends. She felt he needed to reconsider his priorities, to put less energy into his company and into trying to get ahead. The two of them often avoided speaking to each other, and when they did try to talk their conversations quickly degenerated into bickering.

Raj and Kara were suffering from what I call "mis-matched *vasanas*." Like many couples, initially they had been attracted to each other because of their differences. When they had first gotten together, both had believed they had found their missing half. But now those same differences were driving them apart, and their marriage had become a battleground of smoldering resentment.

One Saturday Kara asked Raj to stay home so they could discuss their relationship. She knew their problems could be resolved if Raj would join her spiritual group and start practicing with her. The practices, she thought, would open him to selfless love and make him question what she saw as his relentless ambition. She had tried to talk to Raj about this before, but he had always become furious and accused her of attempting to control him. This time she prepared for the conversation by taking notes while reading a best-selling book about communication techniques. She had learned how to send "I" messages, acknowledge feelings, and clearly state her needs. Armed with these new strat-egies, she felt confident Raj would finally understand the wisdom of her perspective.

But things didn't go as Kara had hoped. She had enthu-siastically launched into her speech, clearly describing her version of the relationship, what her feelings were about the situation, and which of her needs weren't being met.

However, when it was finally Raj's turn to speak he had said he was tired of her attempts to change him—he didn't want to be married to a missionary. Then he had walked out the door. Several hours later, when he had returned, he refused to continue the discussion.

Kara was so invested in her desire to change Raj she couldn't see that she needed to change as well. It took several weeks and a number of conversations with friends and her teacher before she saw her role in the conflict. Gradually, she understood that her campaign to fix Raj and transform him into her ideal husband had nothing to do with either love or her practice of devotion. In her effort to reform her husband, she had forgotten that the foundation of relationship rests on knowing the other person's true self and acting with a commitment to the good of the relationship. She had forgotten about the importance of acceptance. She had forgotten that communication is a two-way street, where both people have a perspective, and that listening is an essential part of communication.

LISTENING WITH THE INTENTION
TO UNDERSTAND

Many conflicts in relationships occur because we're unable to let go of our own perspective and understand the other person's reality. To see beyond our reality—our own desires, opinions, and judgments—we must consciously have an intention to understand another person's point of view. Few of us listen with this aim in mind. Instead, we listen through the filter of our personal and cultural conditioning, without realizing how our conditioning distorts our understanding of others. We listen selectively, paying attention to what resonates with our own desires and preconceptions rather than focusing on the speaker's message. Additionally, as we go through the motions of listening we're often so busy planning what to say next that we barely hear what's said, or our minds are so filled with our own internal self-judgments that we can't focus on the other person.

By contrast, when we listen with curiosity and the desire to truly understand, the other person often senses our attentiveness, opens up, and speaks in a more authentic way. An attitude of care and curiosity can transform a stale interchange into a vital conversation that supports an authentic relationship.

MONITORING ATTENTION

Open listening requires full engagement, but we're so used to multitasking that focused attention is becoming a lost ability—as when two people carry on a conversation over dinner while simultaneously working on their laptops. Sustaining focused listening takes persistent practice.

When someone starts to speak, we must remember that our intention should be to understand the individual. Then as our attention strays, if we observe anything arising in the mind that distracts us we should consciously shift our awareness back to the speaker. This is another form of the practice of observation.

Throughout the conversation, we should sit still and maintain eye contact with the speaker, continue to give them our full attention, and listen with an attitude of curiosity. The value of listening with full attention is illustrated in the following anecdote involving Kara and Raj.

Kara's teacher suggested she observe her internal dialogue when she listened to Raj. That evening he started telling her about a soccer game he had watched with his friends. As Kara observed her mind, she saw she wasn't really listening to him. His words floated in the background; her own thoughts monopolized her attention. *What is wrong with him? I can't believe he wasted an entire afternoon watching a bunch of guys running around a muddy field kicking a ball,* she thought. Then she looked out the window and noticed the glass was dirty and needed to be cleaned.

Once Kara had observed what she was doing, she remembered her intention to truly listen and refocused her attention on Raj, making eye contact with him. Then she saw how excited he looked as he described the game.

Suddenly, it hit her that he really cared about soccer, and she was curious why.

She started asking him about the game, and because her questions stemmed from genuine curiosity she listened to his answers. The two ended up talking for several hours—the most time they had spent together in months. During the conversation, Kara found out, among other things, that Raj had arranged for his company to sponsor a local soccer team and he was helping one of the team's talented players apply for college.

Just by attentively listening, Kara began to see that her picture of Raj as someone driven by money and ambition wasn't quite accurate. She realized she had created a simplistic, fixed, and rather negative image of her husband. Once she began listening to him directly, outside the lens of her own preconceived view, she heard someone who cared about, and was engaged with, the world. Maybe he had changed and she had never even noticed; or maybe she had never really seen him. Regardless of which hypothesis was true, she was finding a side of her husband that she had previously ignored because it had not fit with her idea of who he was.

As Kara reflected on how she communicated with Raj, she saw the humor in their conflict. She longed for him to join her spiritual practice so he could connect with his true self; but in her crusade to fix her husband she had lost touch with her own true self—the source of unconditional love. She had become overly judgmental and had forgotten her basic commitment to support Raj. But the simple act of attentive listening—genuinely trying to understand his perspective without judging—helped her see him more clearly. Even though she meditated daily and practiced devotion in a spiritual community, she had neglected to bring her practice into her conversations with her husband.

During the next few months, Kara worked to become a more attentive listener, and in response her relationship with Raj began to shift. Raj sensed the change in Kara's attitude and felt her love and acceptance of him for who he was. As Raj felt safer in the relationship, he began expressing his feelings more freely and listening to his wife more attentively. Over time, listening became a healing force for the couple's marriage. They were able to drop the defensive shields preventing them from communicating with each other and connect in a way that reinforced their love for each other.

CULTIVATING EMPATHY

A man whose wife had threatened to leave him went to see a counselor. "If you want this relationship to work, you must learn to listen to your wife," the counselor told him.

Several weeks later the man returned and told the counselor he had learned to focus his attention and listen to everything his wife said. "Good," the counselor replied. "Now learn to listen to everything she isn't saying."

When we view others as embodiments of divine essence and listen to them with the intention of understanding their perspectives, we hear more than the literal meaning of their words; we also hear what isn't said and sense the motivations and feelings underlying their words and actions. In this way, we cultivate empathy—the ability to feel other people's experiences *with* them. Our capacity for empathy develops to the degree that we're able to temporarily let go of our own perspective and enter into other people's realities. If we momentarily put aside our own preoccupations, our hearts open and we feel the full presence of others, hearing both what they say and don't say, the meaning beneath the surface of their words.

Empathy is a mother's natural response to her children. For example, when Nora's one-year-old child, who is just learning to walk, fell down and hit her head, immediately Nora felt the pain of the fall and her child's fear. "How scary! Ouch, your head must hurt," she said, picking the child up. A second before, she had been worrying about her credit card bill; but when her child fell she became completely present, devoid of all self-concern and judgment.

She wasn't thinking that her child was clumsy, or lazy for not having learned to walk sooner, or that she should pay more attention to where she's going. When she saw the child fall, she empathized with her and responded spontaneously from her heart.

Although parents often feel empathy for their young children, between adults empathy can be suppressed by judgment. Nora responded empathically to her one-year-old daughter, but she did not react this way when her friend Sarah called to say her husband had filed for divorce. On hearing the news, Nora immediately remembered how, years before, she had warned Sarah against marrying him. She tried to listen to Sarah's story, but most of her attention was focused on validating her own past judgments. With effort, Nora refrained from saying, "I told you so." Instead, she told Sarah the divorce was for the best and she should have gotten out of the marriage years ago. Sarah just needed a friend to listen to her sadness, fear, and anger—to be present with her pain—but Nora's judgments blocked her ability to empathize with Sarah, and her criticism only added to Sarah's suffering.

When we judge other people, we create a barrier to listening and understanding. Instead, we can cultivate empathy toward people by becoming aware of our judgments and stopping them while listening to people speak. If we can do this, the wall blocking understanding disappears, and an opportunity for genuine connection arises. As humans, we all experience the joy of love and the pain of loss, and, as Vedanta teaches, we all share the same divine essence. When we let go of the judgments that reinforce our sense of separateness, we open to the source of empathy—our interconnection with others.

EXERCISES

1. While in the presence of another individual, practice listening to them while viewing them as an embodiment of divine essence. Observe anything arising in your mind that shifts your focus, then return your attention to the speaker. Listen empathically, intent on understanding their feelings as well as the content of their message. Become aware of judgments or opinions that surface for you, then let go of them so you can remain present for the speaker.

2. Set a conscious intention to simply listen for an entire day. As you interact with others, pay attention to what they say; listen fully, without expressing judgments or comments. Notice any changes in the way you feel about yourself when you listen without judging or commenting.

By speaking kindly, we encourage other people to remain open; and by expressing love, we make the world a warmer place.

8

Learning Wise Speech

TO SPEAK AND TO SPEAK WELL ARE TWO THINGS.

A FOOL MAY TALK, BUT A WISE MAN SPEAKS.

—Ben Jonson

MASTERING WISE SPEECH—that is, learning to speak thoughtfully and truthfully in a way that benefits relationships—requires care and discipline. As Swami Chinmayananda observed: "It reflects the intellectual caliber, the mental discipline, and the physical control of the speaker."[1] The words spoken by a well-integrated personality reflect clarity, power, and caring. As such, wise speech has the power to heal: the right words spoken with love can foster a growing relationship or lessen the pain of another's suffering.

THE CHALLENGES OF WISE SPEECH

The challenges involved in learning wise speech are illustrated in the following scenario. Mary occasionally enjoyed a glass of wine with dinner. Then when her husband of forty years was diagnosed with cancer she started having a glass or two every evening. Throughout his long illness, she kept her husband at home and took care of him by herself while continuing to work full time. She had always been the rock in the family—unflappable in a crisis, well-organized, and in control.

After her husband died, Mary's youngest son, Frank, moved in to help her temporarily. During the first night of his stay, Mary fell while going upstairs to the bathroom. When Frank helped her up, he realized she was so drunk she could barely walk. Two days later she missed work because she was too hungover to get out of bed. The next night when she opened a bottle of wine Frank was about to say something about her drinking, but the second he opened his mouth his normally even-tempered mother yelled at him to mind his own business.

Frank was momentarily startled into silence, but he knew eventually he had to talk to her, and he dreaded the conversation. He felt sorry for her; she was obviously still devastated by her husband's death and was so touchy she would be furious with him for even mentioning her drinking. Above all, he had no idea what to say and was afraid the wrong words could make the situation worse.

Frank was understandably hesitant to talk to his mother without first thinking through exactly what to say, as he had already discovered his mother's sensitivity to his words. Indeed, words have power; they can damage or even destroy a relationship. The Talmud describes the tongue as an instrument so dangerous it must be concealed behind the fortress of the mouth and teeth to prevent its misuse.

As Frank learned, finding the right words can be challenging. When speaking about a difficult issue, it's tempting to just start talking, hoping for the best. The problem with this approach is that what spills forth from the mouth may express negative *vasanas* rather than helpful expressions. It's prudent to wait before speaking, taking the time to clear the mind and allow internal dialogue to quiet. In an emotionally charged situation, quieting the mind may require hours or days, but it's time well spent. Before speaking, it is also useful to remind ourselves of our commitment to love and support the other person, and to consciously resolve to speak in a way that benefits the situation.

THE QUALITIES OF WISE SPEECH

The Bhagavad Gita offers specific time-tested guidelines for speaking thoughtfully in a way that benefits rather than harms relationships. Krishna describes the qualities of wise speech: "To offer soothing words; to speak truly, kindly, and helpfully; and to study the scriptures: these are the disciplines of speech."[2]

Soothing Speech

Soothing speech is speech that arises from the heart rather than the intellect. For example, when terrified by a nightmare a child wakes up in the middle of the night crying. Her father rushes into her room and says, "There, there, it's OK. Don't be afraid; it was only a dream." Hearing his soothing speech, his daughter relaxes and quickly falls into a deep sleep. The father's ability to calm his daughter comes not only from his words but from his confidence and love. Because his words are congruent with his inner state, he's able to communicate security and soothe her fears.

Gandhi was a master of soothing speech. He was famous for being able to disarm his enemies with his loving presence and calm words, an ability that enabled him to converse civilly with even his fiercest opponents. A scowling political enemy would arrive to see Gandhi and after a long conversation would emerge transformed, walking arm in arm with him, relaxed and smiling. Gandhi recognized the power of speech that comes from the heart. He is claimed to have said: Nonviolence, the quality of the heart, cannot come from the brain.

Because emotional states are contagious, it's essential to calm ourselves before speaking. When we remember that our intention in speaking is to express our true selves, our words are more likely to arise from the peace and love at the center of our being. While remaining calm, we can clarify our thoughts and express them in a tone that soothes rather than arouses the passions.

Truthful Speech

Truthful speech, in the fullest sense, involves using words in a way that benefits the overall situation and considers their long-term effects. A Jewish tale illustrates the danger of untruthful speech. An influential man with many friends began spreading nasty lies about a local rabbi. Later, when he saw how much he had damaged the rabbi's reputation he felt terrible. He begged the rabbi for forgiveness, asking how he could make amends.

The rabbi told the man, "Take a feather pillow, cut it open, and scatter the feathers to the winds." After carrying out this odd request, the man returned to the rabbi.

"Now," the rabbi told him, "go and gather the feathers." The man soon realized the futility of recovering the feathers and, once again, asked the rabbi what to do.

"Words are like the feathers," the rabbi said. "Once spoken, you never know where they'll land and you can never get them back."

Because untruthful words can harm people and can't be retrieved, speech should be truthful. But truth requires more than factual accuracy. A malicious story about a neighbor may actually be true, but if I pass it along I hurt my neighbor and strengthen my *vasana* of indiscriminate gossip. A more truthful approach would be to consider the consequences of my words and refrain from speaking. In cases where words will do more damage than good, silence can be golden.

Yet in another context, remaining silent could be untruthful and cause more damage than good. For example, when Frank reflected on his hesitation to talk to his mother about her excessive drinking he realized his silence was motivated by fear of her reaction. The rest of the family shared his fear and tiptoed around her drinking, pretending everything was normal. Meanwhile his mother was rapidly going downhill. Frank gradually realized that the family's silence was a kind of lie that allowed his mother to continue drinking without being confronted by the effects of her actions.

Ultimately, Frank decided he had a responsibility to speak up. Truthful speech is essential when it will enhance the greater good of the people involved.

Kind Speech

Kind speech is vital—particularly when communicating something difficult to hear. The more difficult the communication, the easier it is to fall into reactive patterns and express negative *vasanas*. Because in an emotionally charged situation kindness can be forgotten, we need to remain aware not only of our own reactions but also of the other person's feelings. Jesus's advice to treat others as you would like to be treated extends naturally to speech: speak to others as you would like to be spoken to. By remaining aware of the other person's feelings, we can remember to speak kindly, to express love and concern using nonjudgmental words.

A scene from my own childhood illustrating kind speech has stayed with me all these years. I used to go with my mother to a specialty retail shop that sold long embroidered shirts called kurtas. In the shop we sat on benches positioned around a huge, flat, low table. The shop assistant stood in an open attic above us, where the kurtas were stored. After a customer placed an order, the owner called out the item number, and the assistant threw down the packet containing it.

But this particular day the shop was packed with people and the assistant couldn't find the right products. After several mistakes, the owner reprimanded him in a way I had never heard before. His tone was neither angry nor belittling as he said, without a hint of sarcasm: "What is troubling you today? Is everything all right? Please, could you possibly pay more attention to these wonderful people and just follow my instructions? You are such an amazing employee, but today is an off day for you. Let's try this again." And then he laughed.

His voice was so soft and kind his speech sounded like poetry. Witnessing it, I understood for the first time that even in a stressful situation, even when someone is making mistakes, we don't have to become impatient and get angry. We can still speak kindly. We can use the power of speech to say what needs to be expressed without hurting others. As Mother Teresa put it, "Kind words can be short and easy to speak, but their echoes are truly endless."[3]

Kind words encourage open listening. When we feel that others care about us, we can hear what they have to say. If the shop owner had yelled at his assistant, his anger would have only increased the assistant's agitation. Instead, his kind words calmed his employee so he could focus on the task at hand. Many conflicts and misunderstandings can be prevented just by speaking kindly, using nonjudgmental words.

When we use nonjudgmental words while conversing with someone with whom we have a relationship, we will be considerably more successful in persuading them to listen and respond positively and beneficially. This process is illustrated by Frank's reflection on how to approach his mother about her excessive drinking. When Frank finally felt prepared to talk to his mother, he invited her out to dinner so they could have an honest conversation. Two hours before the scheduled dinner, Frank's sister called to say their mother had just been released from the police station after being arrested for driving while intoxicated.

Suddenly Frank felt a tornado of emotions surge through his body: fear for his mother, anger that she had acted so recklessly, panic at his inability to control the situation, and guilt that he had waited so long to talk to her about her drinking. His first impulse was to call her and tell her exactly what he felt—that her drinking was irresponsible, self-indulgent, and reckless—and how terrible she looked, how shocked and appalled his father would be if he could see her, and how angry the family felt at having to deal with her thoughtless behavior on top of their grief over the death of their father. But an inner voice warned him that, although he could unleash his anger by expressing his opinions, his mind was so filled with judgments that his words would only worsen the situation. His mother, already overwhelmed by her own emotions, would hear his words as an attack and react defensively.

Instead of speaking impulsively, Frank decided to act with conscious intention. Rather than express judgments about his mother that would undermine his desire to help her, he decided to describe the situation as he saw it without interjecting his opinions.

He began by saying: "I love you, Mom. I'm feeling extremely concerned about you, and I'd like to do whatever I can to support you right now. I know how hard it is for you losing Dad after all these years." His words contained all the elements of wise speech. They were soothing, truthful, and kind. He also showed empathy by acknowledging his mother's ongoing grief over the loss of her husband.

Frank then moved to the more difficult part of the conversation, saying: "Since Dad's death, your drinking has increased dramatically. Last week I found five empty wine bottles in your laundry basket. Your eyes look bloodshot most of the time, and often I smell liquor on your breath. You've been missing work more and more frequently; now you have a serious traffic violation on your record. Your children are worried about you, and your sister called yesterday to talk about how concerned she is about your drinking." Rather than calling his mother "irresponsible," "reckless," "thoughtless," or "self-indulgent," he focused on observable details resulting from her drinking problem: empty wine bottles, bloodshot eyes, the smell of liquor on her breath, missed work, an arrest for drunk driving, and phone calls from concerned family members.

At last, Frank offered help in a clear, direct manner. He avoided lecturing his mother or giving her a hard sell about the advantages of counseling or AA. He simply said he hoped she would get help; then he handed her a list of resources, including the phone numbers and addresses of counselors, AA groups, grief support groups, and treatment programs. He suggested she think about which options might be most appropriate and offered to listen while she sorted things out. Frank's mother took the paper without saying a word. Frank hugged her; she didn't return his hug, nor did she resist it.

Helpful Speech

Helpful speech aims to promote the highest good. To ensure that speech is helpful when a conversation feels difficult, we can pause for a moment to consider what type of communication would be most beneficial under the circumstances. In one context, we might decide to remain silent and simply listen to the other person's perspective. Another situation might call for a discussion of various problem-solving options. Still another might prompt us to simply enjoy our connection to the other person through a leisurely, meandering conversation.

Alternatively, we may need to calm our minds through observation and reflection before delivering a reply. Often in a highly charged emotional situation, feelings and words become scrambled together in the mind. When we feel emotionally overloaded, angry, or confused, our sense of the highest good can be muddled, in which case the best strategy is to refrain from speaking until we're clear about what will benefit the situation. We can take a break, use mantra chanting and meditation to quiet the mind, or simply observe the mind. While observing, we may hear a chorus of passionate voices urging us to express their point of view. Because a state of emotional arousal can stir up powerful *vasanas* activating ancient habits and desires, it is important at such times to patiently observe the mind without becoming involved in its dramas, allowing it to quiet itself. Just as refraining from stirring murky water eventually allows the mud to settle to the bottom, when we merely observe the mind, turbulent thoughts settle, then consciousness becomes clear and the appropriate words reveal themselves. As Buddha advises, "Better than a speech of a thousand vain words is one thoughtful word which brings peace to the mind."[4]

By consciously considering what would be helpful in each circumstance before speaking, we are less likely to respond in a way that reinforces habitual patterns, as illustrated by the following scenario. When Frank realized that instead of speaking impulsively to his mother he needed to first calm his mind, he reflected on what would be the most beneficial way to express his thoughts to her. He then isolated three points to communicate: his love and concern for his mother, the harmful effects of her drinking, and the availability of help.

Frank understood that his mother would get help only when she was ready, something he couldn't make happen. But because he remained firmly focused on his intention to work for the overall benefit of his family, and he had calmed his mind and reflected sufficiently on how his words could impact the situation, he felt confident in his ability to clearly communicate the most helpful message possible.

For a few weeks after Frank had conveyed these points during their dinner together, his mother continued to drink without responding much to his plea. Frank often felt furious and several times came close to blurting out his opinion of her behavior, but, with difficulty, he stuck to his commitment to only use kind words. A month later his mother started attending a support group for widows; two months later she was drinking less, had made a couple of new friends, and had joined Alcoholics Anonymous. Then she started drinking again—at first just a glass of wine at night, then more—until soon she was drunk every night.

Now Frank decided it was time to back up his words with actions. He moved out of the house, telling his mother he couldn't be around her when she was drinking. A month later she entered treatment. Her decision to seek treatment was her own but had been prompted and supported by Frank's practice of kind speech.

SPEECH ROOTED IN SPIRITUAL PRINCIPLES

Krishna's last recommendation for wise speech was to study the scriptures. Indeed, Vedanta teaches that while the foundation of wise speech rests on seeing the other as an embodiment of the divine and remaining rooted in love, integrating that understanding into speech happens only with consistent discipline—and studying the scriptures is one way to achieve that goal. With repeated contemplation of the scriptures, the teachings become embedded deep in our consciousness, providing a foundation for wise speech. When Hanuman the monkey god spoke, Rama was so struck by his wise words that he thought: *Surely no one could speak with such sweetness without having mastered the*

Vedas, the books of knowledge. Even the heart of an enemy about to strike with a sword would be moved by such speech.

Without sustained study of the scriptures, we easily drift into ego-centered reactions in which our words express habitual patterns rather than what is soothing, true, kind, and helpful. Studying the scriptures deepens our spiritual understanding, allows us to remain focused on the highest good, and permits us to give voice to the divine essence in us all in order to find creative solutions to challenging relationship issues.

Taking the time to speak wisely and from the heart doesn't guarantee that things will go as we wish. I can speak in the most loving way to my teenage nephew, but I can't force him to listen to me or to like what I say. Buddha quotes an ancient saying: "People will blame you if you say too much; they will blame you if you say too little; they will blame you if you say just enough." Then he adds, "No one in this world is free from blame."[5]

Even if people blame us or refuse to listen to us, it's still worthwhile to cultivate wise speech. By learning when to remain silent and refrain from expressing angry or judgmental thoughts, we weaken conditioned patterns; by speaking kindly, we encourage other people to remain open; and by expressing love, we make the world a warmer place.

EXERCISES

1. Practice being silent for three consecutive days. Notice
   the feelings that arise throughout each day and how
   long those feelings stay with you. If you can, a month
   later practice being silent for seven consecutive days
   and notice how fleeting many of your feelings are. This
   understanding will help you refrain from using harmful
   words, allowing you to develop wise speech.

2. In an emotionally charged situation, before speaking
   take time to calm and clear your mind of judgmental
   language. This practice will help you focus on observable details and actions when speaking, rather than
   judgments about them. Notice any differences in
   response from using this approach.

*Understanding a
different perspective opens
us to new possibilities
and provides an
opportunity for more
creative solutions.*

9

Mastering Conflict Resolution

AS THE LOTUS RISES ON ITS STALK UNSOILED
BY THE MUD AND THE WATER,
SO THE WISE ONE SPEAKS OF PEACE AND IS
UNSTAINED BY THE OPINIONS OF THE WORLD.

—Buddha

SINCE CONFLICTS PRESENT one of the major challenges to establishing and maintaining loving and beneficial relationships, learning conflict resolution skills is of utmost importance for sustaining the strength and quality of relationships. To become skilled in resolving conflict, we first need to understand the origins and nature of conflict.

THE ROOTS OF CONFLICT

One lovely April day an elderly man was happily walking down the street when another man came charging out of a café, crashing into him.

"You stupid idiot. Are you blind? Why don't you look where you're going?" he yelled at the old man with whom he had just collided.

The older man bowed to him and said, "My friend, I'm not sure which of us is responsible for this mishap, but let's not waste our valuable time arguing about it. If I ran into you, I beg you to forgive me; if you ran into me, please don't worry about it." He smiled and then, with another bow, walked away.

In less than a minute, the old man had defused a potential conflict and continued on his merry way, enjoying the beautiful spring sunshine. Unfortunately, few people have the skills, presence of mind, and detachment to let things go so gracefully. More commonly two people approach a conflict convinced the truth is on their side, their opposing egos take center stage, the tension rises, and the drama begins. I tell another person I know I'm right; my view is ethical, humane, logical, and practical. If the other individual disagrees with me, it's because that person is mistaken or mean-spirited. Reasonable people, the experts, virtuous individuals all support my view; the longer I argue my position, the more invested I become in being right. And if the other person continues to oppose me I will do everything in my power to make their life miserable.

Meanwhile, the other person tells me how deluded and immoral I am, that I don't care about anyone except myself, and my views will destroy the family and cause the downfall of civilization. Only evil-doers and severely brain-damaged rodents could think the way I do. The longer that other person tries to convince me that they're right, the more entrenched I become in my own position.

In a conflict, when two people try to wear each other down by insisting on the correctness of their respective positions, the odds of one person experiencing a sudden illumination and converting to the other's position is probably zero. One person may threaten, bribe, or out-manipulate the other to get her way, but the person who gives in will harbor resentment, and the relationship will suffer.

Marta and Ursula learned the hard way the futility of trying to overpower each other in a conflict. Shortly after Marta and her husband divorced, she and her three-year-old son, Kai, moved in with her sister Ursula. Ursula immediately stepped in to help with Kai, acting as both his aunt and a second father. Although the two sisters looked so much alike that people often mistook them for twins, temperamentally they were quite different—and their parenting styles reflected these differences.

Marta was a talented painter who encouraged her son's creativity. The house was filled with the colorful results of the many projects Kai had completed with his mother. Kai adored his mother, and she, in turn, doted on him, buying him whatever he wanted. Ursula treated Kai with affection but tended to be stricter, insisting on regular bedtimes, limiting snacks, teaching him to clean up after himself, and making sure he said "please" and "thank you."

For the most part, the sisters' parenting styles seemed to complement each other. Marta recognized that Kai benefited from Ursula's sense of discipline; Ursula was proud of her nephew's creative accomplishments. But after Kai's fourth birthday, when Marta decided it was time to send him to preschool, a conflict between Marta and Ursula arose.

The preschool Marta chose for her son emphasized freedom; the director and teachers believed children flourished with a minimum of rules to interfere with their spontaneous expressions of creativity. When the two women visited the school, however, Ursula was horrified. It took twenty minutes in heavy traffic to get there; and the place seemed chaotic, with children running everywhere, doing whatever they wanted while the teachers stood by calmly ignoring the apparent commotion. Marta, on the other hand, found the place inspiring; the children seemed happy and were offered many choices of creative activities.

Ursula located a more traditional school that emphasized discipline and academics only a couple of blocks away from the house, but Marta refused to visit it. She felt that Kai was her son and therefore she should decide where he went to school. But Ursula, who made a lot more money than Marta, not only loved Kai but helped support him and his mother, and thus was convinced she should have a say in where he went to school. Eventually, Marta gave in and visited the school with her sister but, having already made up her mind, left with a long list of complaints about the place.

The conflict escalated. Ursula pointed out that the neighborhood school would give Kai a foundation in math and language, skills he needed to succeed in the world. When Marta said a four-year-old didn't need to know math, Ursula countered that she was "close-minded and out of touch with reality." Marta, in turn, called Ursula "dogmatic and controlling" and accused her of trying to turn her son into a mindless robot. Ursula suggested that since Marta felt that way, perhaps she and Kai would be better off moving out.

Finally, the sisters stopped speaking to each other. Marta blamed Ursula; and Ursula blamed Marta. Each considered herself a victim of the other's stubbornness, and both spent hours telling stories of victimhood to whomever would listen.

OBSERVING OURSELVES IN CONFLICT

One of the biggest obstacles to resolving conflicts is the fact that people do not want to look at their own contribution to a conflict. As the poet Rumi said, "People of the world don't look at themselves, and so they blame each other."[1] Instead of considering their own role in a conflict, their tendency is to justify the ego's position by focusing on the other person's role. Ursula was so invested in the correctness of her position that she couldn't even imagine the validity of Marta's stance. And Marta was equally sure her sister's point of view was delusional. Each asserted her version of the truth, and meanwhile their relationship deteriorated.

Seeing our own contribution to a conflict requires creating some distance from the situation. The practices of meditation and observation can be tools for this. As we observe our thoughts about our role in the conflict, we may discover an ongoing internal dialogue in which we repeat the same arguments and stories in support of our position. What we are witnessing in such instances is our ego's desperate attempt to justify our *vasanas*. In the heat of conflict, these repetitive tapes sound extremely convincing, but if we listen long enough from the perspective of a detached observer we stop identifying with such justifications.

Observing ourselves in the heat of conflict, while a challenging practice, is extremely valuable. Conflicts can activate our most deeply rooted *vasanas*, and when we watch those patterns without acting on them their power diminishes. Ursula, who prided herself on her rational mind, observed herself generating convincing arguments for the accuracy and superiority of her point of view, though occasionally she couldn't help but notice how she was mentally feeding the conflict. Even after she and her sister stopped communicating with each other, she continued wasting precious time each day engaged in ferocious combat with an imaginary Marta.

After a week of this, it dawned on Ursula that she was not the helpless victim she'd imagined herself to be. She realized that she had chosen to cling to her own point of view and disregard her sister's perspective, and thus she was as responsible for the conflict as Marta.

Seeing ourselves as responsible agents in a conflict provides a sense of freedom and new possibilities. At last we can decide to stop reacting to other people and respond in a way that reflects our higher values. Once Ursula acknowledged her role in fueling the conflict, she realized she could choose how to act. Rather than mechanically reacting from the negative *vasana* that urged her to repay every unkind remark with a nastier one, she could break the cycle of retaliation and stop undermining the deep love between herself and her sister. She could instead be motivated by opportunities to uphold her values of kindness and compassion. At this point, she concluded that the relationship was more important than trying to prove she was right.

HEARING BOTH SIDES OF A CONFLICT

When a disagreement arises, most people react automatically then communications break down, causing both parties to feel unheard and try more vehemently to make their case. Meanwhile, as the two sides become increasingly locked into separate positions, the issue remains unresolved. To move forward, it is essential that both parties listen to, understand, and respect each other's position.

In the case of Marta and Ursula's conflict, for example, upon realizing how important their relationship was to her, Ursula let go of her resentment about Marta's harsh words and began wondering what she could learn if she really listened to her sister. She then apologized to Marta for her role in the conflict and suggested the two of them set up a time to listen to each other.

The basic teaching of Vedanta—that in our essence we are the same—serves as a tool for moving away from polarized positions. When I reflect on the teachings, I remember that just as I am an embodiment of divine essence, so is my "opponent." Just as I am more than my opinions and beliefs, my adversary is also more than her point of view. The true self transcends polarities and recognizes the value of multiple perspectives. It doesn't take one side against another; it isn't progressive or conservative, Catholic or atheist, male or female, practical or imaginative. It goes beyond categories and ideologies. Our true selves are always bigger than any one side in a conflict.

Often when we listen to someone who holds a different position we begin mentally arguing before we even hear their perspective. However, if we can listen to the other person while intent on understanding what they are saying, all the while remembering we don't have to agree or disagree, the conflict no longer feels threatening and becomes interesting. Understanding a different perspective opens us to new possibilities and provides an opportunity for more creative solutions. When we remember this, our former opponent becomes an ally—a source of learning, a guide able to show us another reality, a means for expanding our view of the world.

SETTING GUIDELINES FOR DIALOGUE

In a heated conflict, it helps to set guidelines for dialogue. Before speaking, everyone can commit to participating in the dialogue with the intention of exploring an issue and increasing understanding. A dialogue is not about trying to defend or refute a position; its goal is to promote understanding. One person speaks, while the other listens. The speaker communicates respectfully, using all the elements of wise speech, including lack of blame and judgment. Meantime, the listener refrains from interrupting, monitoring her internal reactions while attempting to openly consider what the other has to say. The listener then simply acknowledges what the speaker has said, without arguing or judging. Once the speaker feels she has been understood, the listener becomes the speaker and the process is repeated.

When Marta and Ursula finally met to talk, Marta took first turn as speaker. Ursula found it extremely challenging to listen without silently arguing with her sister's perspective, but she reminded herself to concentrate on understanding Marta's reality. As her internal dialogue quieted and she focused on listening, the static of her own emotional reactions faded. When Marta finished, Ursula had a much clearer understanding of her sister's point of view.

IDENTIFYING THE UNDERLYING ISSUE
OF A CONFLICT

Resolving a conflict often requires identifying underlying issues that need to be addressed. A proposed solution that addresses only surface problems will probably fail. For example, as Ursula listened to Marta repeatedly asserting her right to select Kai's school, Ursula realized the core issue wasn't which school Kai should attend but rather about how that decision should be made. Marta interpreted Ursula's objection to her choice of school as a challenge to her authority as Kai's mother. She was willing to listen to Ursula's opinion, but she wasn't willing to allow her sister to make the final decision. In addition, Marta felt Ursula's insistence on the importance of discipline was an attack on Marta's style of parenting.

When Ursula spoke, she also expressed frustration at the decision-making process. To her, Marta's disregard of her opinion indicated she wasn't valued. She felt unappreciated; she'd worked hard to help parent Kai and loved him as if he were her own son, yet her point of view was considered irrelevant to the decision.

After both women had taken turns speaking and listening to each other, the tone of the conversation changed. Both felt tremendously relieved to have been heard and understood. Once they had articulated the feelings underlying their conflict, they felt lighter. Marta expressed her appreciation for Ursula's support and love of Kai, and Ursula expressed her admiration for Marta as a mother. They then decided to work toward a solution both could support.

With the underlying issues identified and addressed, the conflict itself—between the values of creative freedom and discipline—now seemed fairly easy to discuss. During the conversation, the sisters realized they actually appreciated each other's values. As a painter, Marta valued creativity, but she also understood the importance of discipline. Without discipline, she never would have developed her artistic skills or even the habit of going to her studio every day to maintain her creative output. And as a teacher, Ursula, while insistent on discipline, relied on creativity in preparing her lesson plans and keeping her students inspired and engaged in the classroom.

PLAN C: FINDING A LARGER PERSPECTIVE

"We can't solve problems by using the same kind of thinking we used when we created them," Einstein once observed.[2] This view provides a valuable lesson regarding conflict resolution.

Most people approach conflicts by arguing from polarized positions, thinking: *It's either plan A or plan B—you give up some of your plan, and I'll give up some of mine. If we can't reach a compromise, I'll force you into accepting my plan; then you'll resent me and try to sabotage the agreement.* But by clinging to one perspective, we remain constricted, blocking all possibilities for a creative solution. To move beyond this deadlock, both parties need to let go of their fixed position and find an alternative perspective—plan C—that is larger and more creative than anything yet discussed.

One way to shift the tone of discussion is by approaching a conflict with playfulness and humor. Playfulness and humor reduce tension, help loosen people's rigid attachment to being right, and encourage creative possibilities to help reframe the conflict.

Once both parties have agreed to work toward a more innovative, win-win solution, it's helpful to identify the essential elements needed for it to succeed, including key points from each person's perspective. For example, after their conversation Ursula and Marta identified several points essential for resolving their conflict over Kai's school. First, both of them needed to be involved in the choice and feel good about the decision. Second, Kai's school had to provide a clearly structured program with a range of creative activities.

Ursula did some research and identified several schools meeting these criteria. When they visited the schools, they brought Kai with them and watched how he interacted with the teachers and students. After visiting four different schools, Ursula, Marta, and Kai all agreed on the same one—a school with a structured art and theater program that also used creative arts to teach music, math, and language skills.

In the end, Ursula and Marta's conflict provided an opportunity for greater connection and intimacy. What began as a disagreement had eventually transformed their relationship and improved their communication. In the process of resolving the conflict, both sisters learned to listen more empathically; as a result, they were less judgmental, more appreciative of each other, and better able to communicate honestly. In addition, the conflict challenged each woman to think about her approach to parenting. Marta began to set more limits with Kai; Ursula became more relaxed and playful with him; and together they worked on parenting collaboratively in a more conscious way.

Not all conflicts have such a happy ending. Many people are unwilling to let go of their own position enough to really listen to another point of view. But if even one person in a conflict makes an effort to implement the principles described in this chapter, he can at least stop the conflict from escalating, reduce the power of their negative *vasanas*, gain practice in relating more skillfully, and plant the seeds for a peaceful resolution in the future.

CULTIVATING FORGIVENESS

As a conflict persists, resentment builds, acting as a psychic pollutant that limits our ability to clearly see the situation. If I feel resentment toward a friend, I see her through a lens of negativity, causing anything she says or does to appear suspicious. If she acts kindly toward me, I think it's because she has some ulterior motive; if she criticizes me, I see it as evidence of her malevolence. As long as my mind is tainted by resentment, I have a narrow, fixed image of her behavior that blocks empathy. I'm incapable of openly listening to her and remain imprisoned in my narrow position.

The antidote to resentment is forgiveness. An attitude of forgiveness allows us to let go of the constricted energy of ill will and resentment produced by conflict. In the process, we let go of our stories and heighten our awareness, which then becomes an ally in observing how we perpetuate our own side of a conflict.

Forgiveness can't be forced. Because the ego-centered self loves to hold on to anger and blame—sometimes for months or even years—we must first observe how we hold on to resentment and feed it with our angry thoughts and stories of victimhood. Then eventually, as we continue to observe ourselves the ego-centered mind exhausts itself, allowing us to see and accept responsibility for our part in the conflict, loosen the *vasana* of resentment, open to the broader perspective of our true selves, and generate compassion for the other person. And because holding on to resentment is painful, it is important to give ourselves this same compassion. Then each time a resentful thought arises, through compassion we can let it go. With practice, forgiveness can become a consciously cultivated habit that frees us from resentment and moves us toward greater freedom.

Buddha graphically described this process of letting go of resentment:

> "He was angry with me; he attacked me; he defeated me; he robbed me." Those who dwell on such thoughts will never be free from hatred. "He was angry with me; he attacked me; he defeated me; he robbed me." Those who do not dwell on such thoughts will surely become free from hatred. For hatred can never put an end to hatred; love alone can. This is an unalterable law.[3]

In the Bhagavad Gita, Krishna lists forgiveness as one of the moral virtues cultivated by a self-realized person. By practicing forgiveness, we reverse the habit of feeding resentment and find greater freedom in our relationships.

Ultimately, forgiveness benefits the person who forgives, as expressed by the following anecdote. Two ex-prisoners of war met many years after their captivity. One of them asked the other, "Have you forgiven them yet?"

The second one replied, "No, never."

"Well, they still have you in prison, don't they?"

As Swami Chinmayananda told us, through the discipline of forgiveness we can eventually develop "an unruffled serenity even in the face of the most powerful opposition and provoking situations."[4]

EXERCISES

1. Think of a conflict you have with another person. Rather than blaming that individual for the conflict, identify your own role in it. Observe specific ways in which you fuel the conflict.

2. Imagine holding a remote control and watching your conflict play out in a video. When you get to an intense scene, hit the Pause key and identify your feelings about the situation. Then replay the scene and, based on the tools you now have, decide what you would say or do differently to resolve the conflict.

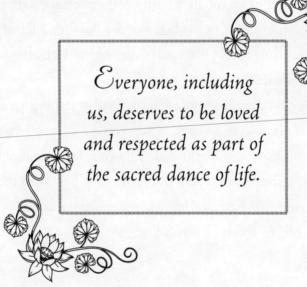

Everyone, including us, deserves to be loved and respected as part of the sacred dance of life.

10

Taking Time to Love

THERE IS MORE TO LIFE THAN INCREASING ITS SPEED.

—Mohandas Gandhi

*T*HE PRACTICE OF RELATIONSHIPS—the cultivation of deep, joyful connections with others—gives us opportunities to transcend our limitations, release our *vasanas* in a mindful, conscious way, and connect with ourselves, as well as to our source of love, power, divinity, joy, and peace. However, the practice of relationships requires time. And in our modern, fast-paced world—an "age of agitation" focused on time-saving devices and high-speed connections—time always seems to be in short supply.

THE AGE OF AGITATION

Almost everyone in this hyperactive age of agitation is driven by the pressure to do more, be more, work more, and spend more in less time, leaving us barely time to check in with ourselves let alone our loved ones. It's as though the train is always about to leave the station, and we're forever running to catch it. Our current anti-mantra is "Hurry, hurry, hurry," which we repeat hour after hour, day after day, until it becomes an ongoing refrain in our subconscious minds, keeping us busy and anxious, as described in the following scenario.

The alarm rings, its annoying sound awakening Cindy. It's 7:00 am and time to get up. A surge of adrenaline speeds through her body, erasing all but a fragment of her dream. It had something to do with her boss, broken equipment, and anxiety. She had been standing in front of a room full of suit-wearing executives wondering what she was supposed to say. Then she remembers: today is the day she has to make a presentation. She reminds herself not to forget the charts. Her mind races between tasks and activities awaiting her—she needs to take the car to the mechanic, set up for the presentation, take her daughter Lucy to her flute lesson, have lunch with her friend Sonya, sit through client appointments, do grocery shopping, go to the school board meeting at 7:00 pm.

She gets in the shower, her mind still reeling off her list of activities on this jam-packed day. She barely notices the warm water on her skin or the smell of the lavender soap. She won't have time to meditate this morning—even though she keeps promising herself she'll somehow find time to start her days more calmly.

The timed automatic coffeemaker has done its job; the coffee is ready to rev her up even more. After two cups she barely tastes, Cindy greets her daughter, who's just gotten up, and kisses her husband on her way out the door, wondering if she has time to stop at the ATM.

At the end of the day, an exhausted Cindy has accomplished an impressive list of tasks, but she's already worrying about all she has to do the following day. Somehow, her world has become one never-ending to-do list. As fast as she finishes one task, two new ones appear; and when those two are done, sixteen urgent items suddenly materialize. Some days she feels exhilarated by all she's accomplished; other days she barely makes it through dinner. Then there are days when the unpredictable happens—her daughter gets sick, the stock market crashes, the power fails, or the roof leaks—and her world spins out of control. At such times, she sees the craziness of the life she's created and vows to slow down and spend more time on what's really important.

Cindy is caught in an all-too familiar trap. Our consumer-driven economy of instantaneous connections and continual change runs on speed and human desire. The power of our *vasanas*, which compel us to satisfy our desires, creates an endless stream of new needs. Not only are we driven by our own inner compulsions to act on our *vasanas*, we are also manipulated by incessant media messages feeding those *vasanas* by telling us we're not good enough and would be more powerful with the newest app; we'd look younger and feel more confident if we could afford the newest skin procedure; and be happier if we could attract the perfect partner. We race through our lives trying to pile up trophies. When we succeed in getting what we want, it's validation that all the effort is worth it. When we fail, it's a sign we need to try harder, do more, go faster.

The body-mind state resulting from this continual race is highly addictive. Infusions of stress-induced adrenaline keep our nervous systems primed and numb us to our deeper feelings. We lose touch with the understanding that we could die at any moment; we are distanced from the fear of the unknown, and the current of deep love that runs through our being is eclipsed by anxiety and grasping. With our numerous meetings and responsibilities, we're too busy to look at our lives in a way that might challenge us to change and too numb to see the urgency of doing so.

We pay a steep price for this behavior. The speed of our minds prevents us from knowing ourselves and others, as well as experiencing our unity with the world. Instead, our ego-created, *vasana*-driven selves engage in a drama we create from our thoughts and feelings. No matter how much we achieve, how much money we make, or how many friends we have, this insecure self who craves approval can never be permanently satisfied and always needs more validation. A subtle but pervasive sense of insecurity runs through our consciousness and propels us to keep moving. In our self-created drama, the character named "me" is always chasing after—but never reaching—an ephemeral future, running faster and faster, oblivious to the wonder of the present moment.

LOSS OF THE PRESENT MOMENT

The artist Georgia O'Keeffe pointed out the necessity of being present to experience and knowing our world, including other people, saying, "Nobody sees a flower—really. It is so small it takes time—we haven't time—and to see takes time, like to have a friend takes time."[1] When we slow down enough to pay attention to our surroundings and circumstances, the world expands and we can see the wonder and the beauty of a flower or a friend, as illustrated by the following scene.

After being diagnosed with high blood pressure, Cindy reluctantly took the advice of a friend and signed up for a five-day silent meditation retreat at a lodge located on a quiet wooded piece of land miles from the city. She spent the first two days of the retreat regretting her decision to attend. Trapped inside her mind with only herself for company, she experienced an incessant stream of thoughts and feelings—worry about all she had to do, memories of things gone wrong, pride about her accomplishments, plans for the future, regrets about the past. Anger, jealousy, fear, pride, happiness, and despair all shaped her thoughts. At some point, she realized how rarely she was present without an ongoing mental commentary determining her reality. And this internal pandemonium was occurring in the silence of a mediation retreat where all she had to do was to sit quietly; how much worse it must be on a pressure-filled day at work! As she reflected on her daily life from the distance of the wooded sanctuary, it seemed insane. She had willingly surrendered control of her life to her tyrannical mind and its never-ending desires. But where was this mind leading her? What really mattered? She thought about how little time she actually spent with her family and friends, and a wave of sadness surged through her body.

By the fourth day, her controlling mind was only making some low-key background noise. As she walked down

the path outside the meditation center, she was aware of everything: the astounding size of a boulder, the breeze on her skin, the rumble of the creek, the way when she walked the trees moved, as if dancing with her. The world, wondrously strange yet familiar, spoke to her intimately as though greeting a long-lost lover. She vowed right then to slow down and pare down her activities to what was essential so she could meditate, spend more time with her family and friends, and be present to enjoy her life.

For the first week after the retreat, Cindy stuck to her resolution. She set aside thirty minutes each morning to meditate, and she made time to spend with her daughter and husband. But then, as if someone cranked up the speed on the treadmill, she began moving faster, trying to keep up with everything demanding her attention. She saw herself, once again, speeding past the people she loved, putting trivial tasks ahead of what truly mattered.

To go against the current of the *vasana*-driven mind takes more than well-intentioned resolutions. As I go through the day, I watch how *vasanas* constantly surface in the form of desires. I would like to go to the concert on Friday, help feed hungry people, get back at my nasty cousin, eat chocolate, rule the universe—or at least get a promotion at work. If I acted on every impulse crossing my mind, I would soon die of exhaustion. Meher Baba observed, "The entire life of the personal ego is continually in the grip of wanting . . . an attempt to seek fulfillment of desires through things that change and vanish."[2] Vedanta shows us that the way to freedom is through awakening to who we truly are, but how can this happen when we're driven by our *vasanas*, running after our desires so fast that we don't taste our breakfast? Resisting the force of indiscriminate desires calls for a serious commitment and a full-fledged battle plan for carrying out that commitment.

CLARIFYING ESSENTIAL VALUES AND ACTIVITIES THROUGH INTROSPECTION

Many of the desires we work to fulfill are superficial and give us only momentary satisfaction. Regular introspection helps put our lives in perspective so we can clarify our essential values.

In the case of Cindy, although she realized she needed to slow down she lacked clarity about how to rearrange her priorities so she could focus on what was truly important to her. Without a clear vision of a life centered on her deepest values and a plan to eliminate the nonessentials, she allowed herself to become a victim of other people's expectations. Like Cindy, many people are aware that something is out of balance in their lives; they want to slow down, but they feel trapped by the necessity of making a living and responding to all the apparent competing demands. Earning money is essential, and meaningful work is a powerful way of contributing to the world, but when work swallows up time so friends and family are neglected something is out of balance.

However, we don't have to go to a meditation retreat to clarify what is essential in our lives. By taking a few minutes each day, or each week, to contemplate what is truly important, we gain perspective on our lives. Asking ourselves the following three questions can help us clarify our essential values and activities:

1. What am I getting back from the energy I expend each day?
2. Is it possible to slow down for a week to connect more from my heart and see what that feels like?
3. If I were to die tomorrow, what would I regret not having done?

The third question is dramatically illustrated by a story about Guru Nanak's teachings to a wealthy man. Guru Nanak gave a needle to a wealthy man, asking him to keep it and return it when he got to heaven. The man readily agreed. When he got home, he handed the needle to his wife, saying, "Please put this needle in a safe place. I have to give it to Guru Nanak when I get to heaven."

"How is that possible?" his wife asked. "You can't take it with you when you die."

Her words shook him to his core. *Of course, she is right,* he thought. *But if I can't take so much as a needle, what can I take?*

He returned the needle to Guru Nanak, saying, "Please take this back and keep it. I just realized I can't take anything with me when I leave this world."

The guru looked at him kindly and replied, "So then, if that's the way it is why do you spend all your time making money?"

Over time, as we become aware of the preciousness of our lives through introspection, our inconsequential desires fade away and our essential values and activities come into focus. For example, Cindy began to transform her life by reflecting for a few moments each day on the kind of life she wanted to create. She worked so hard, but much of that work seemed meaningless, and she rarely found time to be with the people she loved. She realized that if she continued speeding through her days she would never live in a way that expressed her values—and she had even lost touch with what those values were.

As Cindy regularly reflected on her life, she gained clarity about her essential values and activities. She thought about how alive and present she had felt during the final days of the meditation retreat. Then she remembered how during her childhood the world had offered endless beauty and magic. She thought back to the birth of her daughter and the deep love and connection she had felt as she held her for the first time; she recalled the early days of her marriage when she couldn't wait to see her husband at the end of the day. She yearned to again experience such love, magic, and connection.

Once Cindy understood love and connection as core values, she realized she needed to focus on deepening her relationships—including her relationship with her true self. This new clarity about her values served as a touchstone for distinguishing among her various desires so she could focus on activities serving her goal of a life filled with rich, meaningful relationships.

Too many people like Cindy live with only a hazy idea of their life purpose. Clarifying essential values doesn't happen instantly; it's an ongoing process that deepens over time. But when we make time for reflection we set in motion the process that will eventually help us find more balance in our relationships and life experiences.

OBSERVING HOW WE SPEND TIME

Once we clarify the essential values that determine the kind of life we want, we can concentrate on creating that life. If we want a life grounded in our essential values, we need to determine how to use our energy. By observing how we currently spend time, we can assess how much energy we invest in activities that support our essential values and how much we waste on activities having nothing to do with them.

Seeing the reality of how we spend our time can be a powerful motivator. Until we understand how much time we may waste on trivial tasks and activities, we are unlikely to change. But when we identify tasks and activities that no longer serve us, we can eliminate them and free up time for what truly matters. According to a statement attributed to the writer Elbert Hubbard, "The sculptor produces the beautiful statue by chipping away such parts of the marble block as are not needed—it is a process of elimination." In the same vein, eliminating unnecessary tasks and activities shapes our lives in a way that better expresses our true selves.

When Cindy started to analyze how she actually spent her time, she was surprised to find she devoted hours to tasks and imagined obligations having little to do with her essential values or activities. She checked her email five times a day; each week she spent hours in committee meetings, hours gossiping with co-workers, days researching issues for the school board, and hours driving her daughter to various after-school activities instead of actually spending time with her. By evening she was often too exhausted to do anything except collapse in front of the television. She spent little time enjoying other people and even less enjoying her own company.

Although for several years Cindy had tried and failed to simplify her schedule, when she finally looked at how she spent her days she saw how much time was potentially available. Only then did she realize change was truly possible.

CHOOSING ACTIVITIES THAT SUPPORT ESSENTIAL VALUES

Once we've eliminated tasks and activities that drain our energy, we free up time to live in a way that is more congruent with who we truly are. As we start to focus on things we care about, we connect more fully with our true selves and we become more creative and resilient. When activities reflect our essential values, we tap the reservoir of energy that sustains us in times of stress, helps us concentrate more intently on what needs to be done, and allows us to be more fully present with other people.

To start eliminating some of her nonessential activities, Cindy first compiled a list of all her activities that had nothing to do with her essential values, and she chose one to eliminate. She resigned from a committee at work and used the time to walk in the park. Those daily walks energized her, and with one less responsibility she felt calmer and more focused. She was also finally able to establish a practice of regular meditation, getting up twenty minutes earlier each day and meditating for ten minutes. The extra minutes of meditation allowed her to more consciously pursue her other daily activities without feeling so rushed and anxious. At first it took willpower to get up when the alarm went off. But soon she felt the benefits of the meditation, and when she missed a session she noticed she was more scattered throughout the day. Before long she began looking forward to her morning meditation, relishing the stillness in the house and her mental peace.

After a few months, she felt less compelled to check her email and, increasingly bored by the office gossip sessions, started avoiding them. Each increment of freed time energized her further, and because she felt less overloaded she worked more efficiently. Her increased efficiency freed up even more time and energy. In the evenings, instead of watching television she talked to her husband or helped her daughter with her homework.

On weekends, Cindy no longer brought home stacks of work from the office. Instead of holing up in her study, she spent time with her family, reconnected with old friends, and made time for herself. As her priorities shifted, she spent more time with other people and also made more time for herself, listening to music and simply enjoying being alive.

MAKING TIME FOR OURSELVES

Making time for ourselves is not just a nice idea—
something to be done after the essential things are taken
care of. It is indispensable in creating a meaningful life and
vital for cultivating nurturing relationships. Without time
for ourselves, it's easy to lose sight of what's important, forfeit
our connection with our true selves, and feel cut off from
the source of our power, creativity, and love. Living selflessly
doesn't mean ignoring our own needs. When we care for
ourselves, we care for the wisdom, joy, and love essential
for all our relationships; we honor the divine source within
all of us; and we understand that everyone, including us,
deserves to be loved and respected as part of the sacred
dance of life.

We can choose to honor our lives by slowing down and
nurturing awareness, or we can allow our lives to be run by
ancient, unconscious patterns. In her poem "When Death
Comes," Mary Oliver powerfully expressed that choice.
"When it's over," she wrote, "I want to say: all my life I was
a bride married to amazement. . . . I don't want to end up
simply having visited this world."[3]

Our lives are a gift, and we can choose to squander that
gift by remaining trapped in egocentric delusions driven

by our *vasanas*, or we can choose to open our hearts to
the mystery of our existence, to live as a "bride married to
amazement."

EXERCISES

Do the following exercises, in any order you wish, over a
period of three weeks.

1. Pick a day and cook, or do any chore in the kitchen,
   with total mindfulness, observing your breathing as you
   go about the task.

2. Walk slowly and mindfully for twenty minutes. As
   you walk, be aware of your body and of the sights and
   sounds you experience, observing how this walking
   meditation differs from the way you ordinarily perceive
   the world when you walk.

3. Walk in nature or in your yard. Pick a tree you connect
   with, and fully experience all aspects of it, even embrac-
   ing it if you feel adventurous.

Once we know ourselves as sources of love, joy arises, along with wisdom and a sense of freedom, while relationships become spontaneous expressions of love.

AFTERWORD

The Fruits of Practice

THE AWAKENING PRACTICES discussed in this book—observation, meditation, chanting mantras, devotion, action, open listening, wise speech, conflict resolution, values clarification, and creating a life based on values—require work and commitment. Ultimately, however, the benefits of these practices far outweigh the effort they require. When we engage in these practices over time, regularly and devotedly, entrenched habitual patterns lose their power and start to diminish, and the joy and clarity ordinarily obscured by layers of conditioned behavior begin to penetrate our daily awareness. As the lotus of our true selves emerges into consciousness, all our relationships—with ourselves and the rest of the world—are transformed.

The practice of relationships builds upon this work. One gift of this practice is a focused mind. Our ability to concentrate increases; we can be more present with other people; and increasingly our minds become less caught up in anxieties and fantasies allowing us to be present in the moment without replaying the past or worrying about the future. Then we can respond to people more clearly—with wisdom, compassion, and creativity.

The practice of relationships also asks us to be present to the full play of emotions. As we permit our hurt, anger, jealousy, fear, and shame to come into consciousness, we develop the capacity to experience challenging emotions without acting on them; we become less reactive and more patient; we learn to accept ourselves and treat ourselves kindly. And then we extend that acceptance and kindness to other people.

On the other hand, if—to protect ourselves from the discomfort of our feelings—we avoid being fully present in relationships, we limit the mind's natural expansiveness, lose our power as embodiments of divine essence, and shut down the expression of our true selves. When we consciously remain open to ourselves and others both mentally and emotionally, we wear away the *vasanas* that obscure our true nature; we detach from beliefs, thoughts, and expectations; and we allow our love to shine forth.

As the innate qualities of our true selves emerge, we find treasures vastly more precious than possessions or achievements. Once we know ourselves as sources of love, joy arises, along with wisdom and a sense of freedom, while relationships become spontaneous expressions of love.

When we understand that we all share the same divine essence, we know that whatever we do affects others and whatever others do affects us. In our world of interconnection, each expression of kindness or generosity touches other people. Thus the practice of relationships has the potential to transform our families, communities, and even our world, awakening us to our deep interconnectedness. Increasingly, we relate to people with love and care, the lotus of our hearts opens, and the world becomes a kinder, more beautiful place.

NOTES

INTRODUCTION

1. Eknath Easwaran, trans., *The Upanishads* (Berkeley: Blue Mountain Center of Meditation, 1987), 192–93.

CHAPTER ONE

1. Swami Chinmayananda, trans., *Kathopanishad* (Mumbai, India: Central Chinmaya Mission Trust, 2008), 115.
2. Ramana Maharshi, *The Spiritual Teachings of Ramana Maharshi* (Boston: Shambhala Publications, 1988), 11.
3. Eknath Easwaran, *Upanishads*, 93.
4. Kahlil Gibran, *The Prophet* (London, England: Arrow Books, 1991), 12.
5. Jelaluddin Rumi, "The Minute I Heard My First Love Story," in *The Essential Rumi*, trans. Coleman Bark (Edison, NJ: Castle Books, 1997), 106.

CHAPTER TWO

1. Swami Chinmayananda, *Self Unfoldment* (Mumbai, India: Central Chinmaya Mission Trust, 2007), 41.
2. Swami Chinmayananda, *Bhagavad Gita* (Mumbai, India: Central Chinmaya Mission Trust, 2008), 62–63.
3. Walt Whitman, "Song of Myself," in *Leaves of Grass* (New York: Simon & Schuster, 2006), 105.
4. Thich Nhat Hanh, *Anger* (New York: Riverhead, 2001), 165.
5. Swami Chinmayananda, *Bhagavad Gita* (2011), 61.
6. Ibid., 28.

7. Albert Einstein, letter of condolence to Robert S. Marcus, 1950, www.lettersofnote.com.

CHAPTER THREE

1. Swami Chinmayananda, *Discourses on Mandukya Upanishad* (Mumbai, India: Central Chinmaya Mission Trust, 1990), 244.

CHAPTER FOUR

1. Martin Luther King, quoted in Jack Kornfield, *The Wise Heart: A Guide to the Universal Teachings of Buddhist Psychology* (New York: Bantam, 2009), 394.
2. Swami Chinmayananda, *The Art of Living* (Mumbai, India: Central Chinmaya Mission Trust, 2008), 34.
3. Swami Chinmayananda, *Bhagavad Gita* (2011), 23.
4. Jelaluddin Rumi, quoted in Linda J. Ferguson, *Path for Greatness: Spirituality at Work* (Victoria, Canada: Trafford, 2000), 51.

CHAPTER FIVE

1. St. Bernard, quoted in Eknath Easwaran, *The Bhagavad Gita for Daily Living,* vol. 2 (Berkeley, CA: Blue Mountain Center of Meditation, 1988), 357.
2. Jelaluddin Rumi, "Gamble Everything for Love," in *The Essential Rumi,* trans. Coleman Bark (Edison, NJ: Castle Books, 1997), 106.

CHAPTER SIX

1. Confucius, *The Analects,* trans. James Legge (Whitefish, MT: Kessinger Publishing, 2004), IV.3.
2. Pablo Neruda, "Sonnet XVII," in *100 Love Sonnets,* trans. Stephen Tapsott (Austin, TX: University of Texas Press, 1986), 39.

3. Hafiz, "The Gift," in *The Gift: Poems by Hafiz*, trans. Daniel Ladinsky (New York: Penguin Compass, 1999), 83.

CHAPTER EIGHT

1. Swami Chinmayananda, *Bhagavad Gita* (2008), 82.

2. Eknath Easwaran, *The Bhagavad Gita for Daily Living*, vol. 2 (Berkeley, CA: Blue Mountain Center of Meditation, 1985), 346.

3. http://forusa.org/blogs/for/peace-quotes-mahatma-gandhi.

4. Eknath Easwaran, trans., *The Dhammapada* (Berkeley, CA: Blue Mountain Center of Meditation, 2003), 104.

5. Ibid., 148.

CHAPTER NINE

1. Camille and Kabir Helminsk, *Rumi Daylight: A Daybook of Spiritual Guidance* (Putney, VT: Threshold, 1994), 119.

2. Albert Einstein, quoted in Steven Covey, *The 7 Habits of Highly Effective People: Powerful Lessons in Personal Change* (New York: Simon & Schuster, 1989), 42.

3. Easwaran, *Dhammapada*, 78.

4. Swami Chinmayananda, *Bhagavad Gita* (2008), 14.

CHAPTER TEN

1. Georgia O'Keeffe, An American Place exhibition catalog (1944).

2. Meher Baba, *Discourses*, vol. 1 (Ahmednagar, India: Avatar Meher Baba Trust, 2011), 27.

3. Mary Oliver, "When Death Comes," in *New and Selected Poems*, vol. 1 (Boston: Beacon Press), 10.

ABOUT THE AUTHOR

SHUBHRAJI, originally from India, is a contemporary Vedanta teacher with universal appeal. After taking an early interest in the ancient nondualistic philosophy of Vedanta, at age fourteen she became a disciple of the renowned Vedanta master H. H. Swami Chinmayananda, with whom she studied for twenty years.

Presently based in Woodstock, New York, Shubhraji teaches and travels throughout the United States, Asia, and Europe. Using the Bhagavad Gita, the Upanishads, and other Sanskrit texts, she lectures on such topics as the art of relationships, spiritual unfoldment, meditation in daily life, the secret to success, and managing the mind. She also conducts related programs in institutions ranging from business schools to spiritual centers.

For more information, please visit:

inthelotusoftheheart.com
and
http://www.namahom.org/